English for Business Studies

Teacher's Book

SECOND EDITION

English for Business Studies

A course for Business Studies
and Economics students

Teacher's Book

Ian MacKenzie

CAMBRIDGE
UNIVERSITY PRESS

PUBLISHED BY THE PRESS SYNDICATE OF THE UNIVERSITY OF CAMBRIDGE
The Pitt Building, Trumpington Street, Cambridge, United Kingdom

CAMBRIDGE UNIVERSITY PRESS
The Edinburgh Building, Cambridge CB2 2RU, UK
40 West 20th Street, New York, NY 10011–4211, USA
477 Williamstown Road, Port Melbourne, VIC 3207, Australia
Ruiz de Alarcón 13, 28014 Madrid, Spain
Dock House, The Waterfront, Cape Town 8001, South Africa

http://www.cambridge.org

First published 1997
Second Edition 2002
Reprinted 2003

Printed in the United Kingdom at the University Press, Cambridge

Typeface Minion (*Adobe Systems Incorporated*) 10/13pt.   *System* QuarkXPress® [OD&I]

A catalogue record for this book is available from the British Library

ISBN 0 521 75286 8   Teacher's Book
ISBN 0 521 75285 X   Student's Book
ISBN 0 521 75287 6   Audio Cassette Set
ISBN 0 521 75288 4   Audio CD Set

Ian MacKenzie teaches at the Haute École de Gestion, Lausanne.

Contents

Thanks and acknowledgements

I would like to thank my editors, Will Capel and Alison Silver, for patiently showing me how to turn my material into a coherent and widely usable course. Alison is also largely responsible for the errorlessness of this Second Edition.

I have to thank my students in Lausanne in the late 1980s, from whom I learnt quite a lot about business, and their successors in the 1990s, on whom I tried out and refined a lot of this material.

I would also like to thank the people who piloted part of this material in schools, colleges and universities in a number of different countries. This Second Edition has benefited from the comments of numerous teachers who used the First Edition. My thanks go to all concerned.

For the listening material, special thanks are due to Julian Amey of the Department of Trade and Industry; Kate Barker of the Confederation of British Industry; Sarah Brandston; Lillian Chew; Professor Jean-Christian Lambelet, Gabriel Mangano and Marc Keiser, all of Lausanne University; Gillian Lewis of Nestlé; Denis MacShane M.P.; Richard Mahoney of J. P. Morgan, New York; Steve Moody of Marks & Spencer, Cambridge; Max Pocock of Leica; Alan Severn of Arcam; Professor Ajit Singh of Cambridge University; Jogishwar Singh of Tégé; and Will Capel of CUP. I owe a special debt to Jean-Pierre Rosset of Lausanne University, who provided a recording studio for some of the interviews, portable tape recorders for some of the others, and the equipment, the expertise, and a great deal of his time, to edit the recordings. Tony Garside and Tim Douglass then performed digital wizardry on the tapes I provided them with: the recordings are no longer 'authentic', they are much better than that!

For the Second Edition, my thanks go to Professor Jared Diamond of UCLA, Chris Peters of the Cambridge Arts Picture House, and Ed Coombes of Cambridge Capital Partners. The new recordings were expertly made and edited by Pete Kyle, and the cassettes and CDs were again edited by Tony Garside and Tim Douglass.

Marc Keiser, Gabriel Mangano and Pablo Ibarrola are responsible for much of the Glossary.

Jayshree Ramsurun expertly handled all the permissions and found all the photographs for the First Edition, while Callie Kendall did the same for the Second Edition. Ruth Carim did the proof-reading.

I must also thank the designers and production staff, and everybody else involved: producing a language course is truly a collaborative exercise.

The author and publishers would like to thank the following for permission to reproduce the commercials in Unit 11 on the recording: HDM Linx/Continental for the commercial for Continental Airlines; What Hi-Fi?/Complete Marketing Communications for the commercial for *What Hi-Fi?*; Mamma Amalfi/Pelican Group for the commercial for Mamma Amalfi.

I would like to dedicate this book to Alex, Charlotte and Elliot, any of whom might yet end up as a business student, probably speaking several more languages than I can manage.

Summary of unit contents

Unit 1, **The three sectors of the economy**, contains an extract from David Lodge's novel *Nice Work* about the complexity of the economic infrastructure, and an extract from a magazine interview with the economist J. K. Galbraith and a recorded interview with the British Member of Parliament Denis MacShane, both about the future of manufacturing industry in the 'advanced' countries.

Unit 2, **Management**, contains a text defining management, an extract from Robert Cringely's book *Accidental Empires* about IBM's system of management, and an interview with Steve Moody, the manager of a Marks & Spencer's store.

Unit 3, **Company structure**, includes a text about different organization structures, an extract from a talk by Jared Diamond about the best way to organize companies, and speaking and writing exercises about the advantages and disadvantages of working for large and small companies.

Unit 4, **Work and motivation**, has a text which summarizes various theories of motivation, and another extract from the interview with Steve Moody, in which he explains how he motivates his staff, and a case study about motivation.

Unit 5, **Management and cultural diversity**, contains a text about cultural differences in different parts of the world, and a number of discussion exercises enabling learners to consider their own cultural beliefs.

Unit 6, **Recruitment**, considers how companies recruit staff, and how business students should go about finding their first job. It also includes advice about writing CVs, and an interview with Gill Lewis, formerly director of human resources at Nestlé, who talks about women in management.

Unit 7, **Labour relations,** has another interview with Denis MacShane, about the role of trade unions, an extract from Bill Bryson's book *Notes From a Small Island* about a trade union, and a text about labour relations in different countries.

Unit 8, **Production**, has exercises about capacity and inventory decisions in production management, a text about the just-in-time production system, an interview with Alan Severn, the quality manager at Arcam Ltd, a producer of hi-fi equipment, and a role play about a product recall.

Unit 9, **Products**, contains a text about product and branding policy, and an interview with Jogishwar Singh of Tégé, a company launching a new fast-food product, and writing and speaking exercises about vending machines and m-commerce, the use of mobile phones to operate vending machines.

Unit 10, **Marketing**, includes a text defining marketing, and a further extract from the interview with Steve Moody of Marks & Spencer, about a hypothetical marketing failure and the possible remedies, and a case study about market research.

Unit 11, **Advertising**, has a text about how companies advertise, a questionnaire concerning whether companies *should* advertise, examples of radio commercials, and an exercise requiring the learners to make their own radio commercial.

Unit 12, **Promotional tools**, includes a second extract from the interview with Jogishwar Singh, in which he discusses the promotional strategy used in the launch of Fresh Fries, and a text and case study about promotional tools.

Unit 13, **Accounting and financial statements**, contains a text defining different types of accounting, an interview with Sarah Brandston, an American tax accountant, who talks about her job, and an exercise based on authentic financial statements from Nokia, the mobile phone manufacturer.

Unit 14, **Banking**, comprises a text defining different types of banks, and a role play in which the learners have to convince a bank to lend them money to develop a business.

Unit 15, **Stocks and shares**, incorporates a text about how companies issue stocks and shares and why people buy them, an extract from a television financial news report, and exercises on the vocabulary of financial markets.

Unit 16, **Bonds**, contains a text and an interview with Richard Mahoney of J. P. Morgan bank, both explaining the use of bonds. There is also a short extract from Tom Wolfe's novel, *The Bonfire of the Vanities*.

Unit 17, **Futures and derivatives**, includes a text about financial derivatives, an extract from a talk by Lillian Chew, a financial writer and journalist, about their dangers, and an extract from Michael Lewis's book *Liar's Poker*, about selling options and futures.

Unit 18, **Market structure and competition**, has a text about market leaders, challengers and followers, and exercises about monopolies, oligopolies, cartels, and so on.

Unit 19, **Takeovers, mergers and buyouts**, consists of discussion exercises about takeovers, an interview with Max Pocock of Leica, in which he explains why the company was formed by a merger, a text about leveraged buyouts, and a writing exercise practising connectors, based on the Vodafone/ Mannesmann takeover.

Unit 20, **Efficiency and employment**, consists of an interview with Kate Barker, a member of the Bank of England's Monetary Policy Committee, about labour market flexibility, and an article from the *Financial Times* about employment patterns.

Unit 21, **Business ethics**, includes a text about the social responsibility of business, and a discussion exercise requiring the students to give their opinions on various ethical issues related to business.

Unit 22, **The role of government**, contains a discussion about the responsibilities of government, and two texts giving the opposing views of two well-known economists, J. K. Galbraith and Milton Friedman. There is also an interview with Julian Amey of the British Department of Trade & Industry, about the ways in which governments can help companies to export.

Unit 23, **Central banking, money and taxation**, has an interview with an economist, Gabriel Mangano, about the functions of central banks, and whether they should be independent from government, and a text and discussion and writing exercises about taxation.

Unit 24, **Exchange rates**, contains both a text and an interview with Jean-Christian Lambelet, an economist, about the advantages and disadvantages of fixed and floating exchange rates.

Unit 25, **The business cycle**, incorporates both a text and an interview with Kate Barker about the causes of the business cycle.

Unit 26, **Keynesianism and monetarism**, includes a text and an extract from the interview with Kate Barker about whether the government can or should intervene in the business cycle.

Unit 27, **International trade**, consists of a text about the growth of international trade and the decline of protectionism, an interview with Ajit Singh of Cambridge University about the advantages and disadvantages of free trade, and the related issue of unemployment in industrialized countries, and a case study about banana exports.

Unit 28, **Economics and ecology**, contains a discussion exercise involving the learners' views regarding ecology, an interview with Marc Keiser, an ecologist, about a system for measuring the environmental impact of manufacturing processes and consumer goods, and an article from the *Financial Times* about a futures market for sulphur dioxide and carbon dioxide emissions.

Unit 29, **Information technology and electronic commerce**, contains an article from *New Scientist* by Ian Angell, the Head of the Department of Information Systems at the London School of Economics, about the dangers of IT, an interview with Chris Peters, a cinema manager, about marketing via the internet and e-mail, and a role play about traditional retailing and e-commerce.

Unit 30, **Entrepreneurs and venture capital**, contains an interview with Ed Coombes, who raises capital for new companies, and a text about entrepreneurs.

Introduction

English for Business Studies is an upper-intermediate to advanced level reading, speaking, listening and writing course for learners who need to be able to express the key concepts of business and economics in English.

The **aims** of *English for Business Studies* are:

- to present learners with the language and concepts found in newspaper and magazine articles on business and economics, and in company documents;
- to develop reading skills and give practice in the comprehension of business and economic texts;
- to provide listening practice in the fields of business and economics;
- to provide learners with opportunities to express business concepts themselves, by reformulating them in their own words while synthesizing, summarizing, analysing, criticizing and discussing ideas.

Unit structure

Most of the units contain three components:

1   An informative main reading text on an important issue, generally preceded by preparatory discussion questions and sometimes a vocabulary exercise, and followed by comprehension and vocabulary exercises and discussion activities.

2   *Either* listening exercises on an authentic interview with a business person or economist, *or* a shorter authentic reading passage, accompanied by exercises.

3   An additional case study, role play, discussion activity or writing exercise.

This structure, however, is not followed slavishly, the aim being to strike a balance between regularity and variety.

Rationale

The **main reading passage** in most units is a synthetic text designed to give an overview of a particular topic. As well as introducing crucial business and economic concepts, these texts have a high density of relevant technical vocabulary. They are designed to spare teachers (and learners) the task of finding for themselves the wide range of newspaper or magazine articles, or texts from other sources, that would be necessary to cover all the requisite ground.

But learners also need exposure to the authentic language of company documents, books, and newspaper articles, designed for particular groups of native speakers, with all their puzzling idiomatic variety and topical references. Thus there are also short extracts from **authentic sources** such as newspapers, books about business and economics, fiction, and so on.

There are **authentic interviews** with a company director, a quality manager, a human resources manager, a store manager, an accountant, a bond dealer, an ecologist, several economists, a financial journalist, a British Member of Parliament, and others. The interviewees include British and American native speakers, and non-native speakers from Germany, Italy, Switzerland, India and Malaysia. Very little of the English that international business people hear in their professional lives is spoken by native speakers, so it is important that learners get used to hearing non-native speakers of English, as well as a variety of native speaker accents.

Approach to the units

The main reading passages are generally preceded by discussion questions. With a teacher and learners familiar with the topic – business school students or practising business professionals – such a preliminary discussion activity can easily be extended to last for much of a lesson, with the teacher eliciting information from the learners, and guiding the discussion according to the content of the text, thereby preparing for and greatly simplifying the subsequent reading task. (Depending on time constraints, the reading passages could also be assigned as homework.)

Nearly all the discussion activities are designed to be done by pairs or small groups of learners, according to the teacher's preferences. Although it is not printed on every page, the instruction **'Discuss in pairs or small groups'** is implicit.

Together, the texts, interviews and vocabulary exercises build up to a fairly thorough collection of business and economic terms, the most important of which are collected in a glossary at the back of the book, with translations into French, German, Italian and Spanish.

The main reading passages are followed by comprehension exercises and vocabulary work (again, for pair or group discussion) on the information and ideas presented in the text. Exercise types include open-ended questions, true/false statements, multiple-choice, matching, sentence completion, and summarizing.

The comprehension and vocabulary exercises are followed by oral activities, including role plays and activities which give the learners the opportunity to discuss the ideas in the text and to defend and develop their own points of view.

The listening sections also include comprehension, vocabulary and discussion activities.

There is additional language practice material (on numbers, word stress, word groups, describing graphs, and so on) at the back of the book.

The units are grouped according to subject matter: an introductory unit, followed by units on management, production, marketing, finance, and economics. The different groups of units are not graded in terms of difficulty, and so need not necessarily be followed in the printed order, but vocabulary items and concepts included in earlier units are not glossed when recycled in later ones. This Teacher's Book contains four **assessment tests**, which can be done after the units on management, marketing, finance, and economics.

Each unit is designed to provide two or three hours' work. The book almost certainly offers more than enough material for a two-hours-a-week course lasting a single academic year.

This Teacher's Book contains guidance on using the material, answers to the exercises, and tapescripts of the listening material. You have permission to photocopy pages which have the following wording: © Cambridge University Press 2002.

Introduction to the Second Edition

The most obvious difference between this new edition of *English for Business Studies* and the original is the addition of two new units. Information technology has spread to such an extent since the book was first written that it needs to be treated in more detail, hence Unit 29. There is also a new unit on entrepreneurs and venture capital. There is an additional authentic text in Unit 7, and more recent authentic texts in Units 20 and 28, both found by searching the Global Archive in the *Financial Times'* website (www.ft.com). Although coursebooks such as this are designed to save teachers the trouble of finding newspaper articles about business subjects, the arrival of internet newspaper archives makes searching much easier. Articles complementing any unit of this book are now easy to find and download.

The world of business and economics does not stand still, and various developments since the mid-1990s made it necessary to update certain units. This applied particularly to the material on banking, central banking and exchange rates. There are also new financial statements in the unit on accounting.

There are new discussion activities in Units 3, 5 and 12, role plays in Units 8 and 29, and a new case study in Unit 27. This Teacher's Book also points to pertinent role plays and discussions in *Business Roles*, *Business Roles 2*, and *Decisionmaker*, photocopiable resource books published by Cambridge University Press. There are additional writing exercises in Units 3, 9 and 23. There is now a sample curriculum vitae or resume in the Student's Book, in Unit 6. The glossary in the Student's Book has been updated to include the new material. The Teacher's Book now has lists of new vocabulary for each unit.

The CDs and cassettes now include a listening exercise for Unit 3, and for the new units. The listening text in Unit 12 remains unchanged, although the exercise in the Student's Book is different. The listening text in Unit 23 has been slightly shortened, and minor changes have been made to Unit 15 and to Exercise 3 in the Language reference section.

I would like to thank all the users of the First Edition who took the time to comment on it, and welcome any comments on this edition, by post to me, c/o ELT at the CUP address in Cambridge, given on the imprints page, or via www.cambridge.org/elt.

Unit 1 | The three sectors of the economy

As mentioned in the Introduction, the units in the Student's Book are grouped according to subject matter: management, production, marketing, finance, and economics. This first introductory unit is more general. It covers a lot of basic vocabulary concerning developed economies, much of it in an extract from a well-known British novel. It also discusses the evolution of the economy of most of the older industrialized countries, with the decline of manufacturing industry and its replacement by services. There is an extract from a magazine interview with an economist and an interview with a British Member of Parliament on this issue. Task **1a**, based on the photograph, provides a good warm-up activity.

An important point: **virtually all the activities in this and the succeeding units can be done in pairs, and then checked with the whole class**. Here this applies to describing the photo in **1a**, classifying the activities in **1c**, answering the questions in **2a** and **2b**, writing the summary in **2c**, and so on.

1 The economic infrastructure

1a Vocabulary

The photo clearly shows a large factory (the Unilever factory in Warrington, England) in the centre, with more factories, industrial units, or warehouses in the top right-hand corner. The large factory seems to include some office buildings. Also visible are agricultural land (in the background; the land in the foreground doesn't appear to be cultivated), a river, a railway and several roads, and housing, perhaps with a school in the centre of the housing estate top left.

1b Reading

> **ANSWER**
>
> The text suggests that most people take for granted the amazing complexity of the economic infrastructure.

Vocabulary notes You probably have to be British to understand 'pebble-dashed semis'. A *semi-* is a semi-detached house, almost a symbol of suburban middle-class life. *Pebble-dashed* means that the bricks are covered with lots of small stones stuck in a thin layer of cement.

It should be pointed out to German speakers that a *warehouse* in English is not the same as a *Warenhaus* (department store) in German; and to French speakers that *inhabit* is the English equivalent of *habiter*, and not the negative *inhabité*.

A possible additional exercise related to this text would be to describe other processes, along the lines of Lodge's description of all the activities that precede boiling water in a kettle. For example, what has been done that enables you to pick up and use a pencil, or brush your teeth, or look in a mirror, and so on.

1c Comprehension

> **SUGGESTED ANSWERS**
>
> 1 Tiny fields (the primary sector), factories (the secondary sector), and railways, motorways, shops, offices, and schools (the tertiary sector).
>
> 2 <u>Primary sector</u>
>   digging iron ore
>   mining coal
>   <u>Secondary sector</u>
>   assembling

building
cutting metal
laying cables
milling metal
pressing metal
smelting iron
welding metal

<u>Tertiary sector</u>
advertising products
calculating prices
distributing added value
maintenance*
marketing products
packaging products*
pumping oil*
transportation

* Some of these answers are open to discussion. For example, if maintenance involves cleaning office floors, this is a tertiary service, but if it involves replacing broken windows or overhauling machines, this is closer to building or construction, and should consequently be considered a secondary sector activity. Similarly, *designing* product packaging is a tertiary sector service, but the physical activity of packaging products can be considered part of the production process, which is of course part of the secondary sector. If pumping oil is understood as extracting oil by pumping water into bore holes, this is a primary sector activity, but if it is understood as pumping oil to or from a refinery, it is a tertiary sector transport activity.

3   Other primary sector activities include farming (agriculture), fishing and forestry.
Other secondary sector activities include manufacturing, transforming and processing.
Other tertiary sector activities include financing, designing and retailing.

1d Discussion

This activity is designed to get learners thinking about the issue of the future of manufacturing in industrialized countries, and the growth of the service sector, for the next part of this unit.

2 Manufacturing and services

2a Reading

ANSWERS

1   Because they think it will lead to unemployment.
2   Designing goods, persuading people to buy them; arts and entertainment.
3   No, because it is a natural, progressive and inevitable development.

2b Listening 🔊

ANSWER

Denis MacShane quite clearly disagrees with Galbraith.

TAPESCRIPT

Interviewer Denis MacShane, do you agree with the people who say that manufacturing industry will inevitably decline in what we call the industrialized countries?

Denis MacShane I think manufacturing will change, convert itself. There are many new products that have to be invented to serve new needs, and they *can* be made in the advanced countries because in fact the technology of production means you need very little labour input. I'm holding in my hand a simple pen that British Airways gives away to its passengers. It is made in Switzerland, a pen, a low-tech product, made in Switzerland, with the highest labour costs in the entire world, and British Airways, a British company, having to pay in low value pounds, is buying from Switzerland a manufactured product. Now what's going on here? It seems to me that the Swiss – and they also manage to do it with their watches, the famous Swatch – have stumbled on a new secret, which is how to make low-tech products, sell them profitably, but actually make them in a country where in theory there should be no more manufacturing, and if you look at any of the successful economies of the 1990s, they all have a strong manufacturing component.

Interviewer Which countries are you thinking of?

Denis MacShane I'm thinking of the dynamic Asian economies, all based on manufacturing, I'm thinking indeed of the United States which now has created for example a new computer, high-tech computer industry, its car industry is coming right back in America. America is a giant manufacturing economy, which is why it is still the richest nation in the world, so I am extremely dubious of the theorists who say that manufacturing has no future in the advanced industrialized countries.

English for Business Studies Second Edition
© Cambridge University Press 2002

ANSWERS

1 Because there are many new products that have to be invented to serve new needs.

2 Because these countries have production technology that requires very little labour input.

3 Precisely because it requires very little labour input.

4 The conventional theory is that the most important cost in manufacturing is labour, and wages and salaries in Switzerland are the highest in the world. (As is the cost of living!)

5 Because the pound sterling has, over the years, lost a great deal of value against foreign currencies, especially the Swiss franc.

6 It has a successful manufacturing economy, including its computer and car (automobile) industries.

7 1 B   2 D   3 A   4 E   5 C

Note After listening to some of the interviews in this book (though certainly not this one), you might be tempted to ask 'What is the most common word in spoken English?', to which the answer would of course be 'Er…'. The tapescripts do *not* include all the ers, hesitations, false starts and repetitions of the speakers.

2c Writing

A POSSIBLE SUMMARY

Galbraith says that manufacturing industry will inevitably decline in the advanced industrial countries, and be replaced by design, advertising, entertainment, and so on. MacShane says that manufacturing will change, and make new products with new technology.

New words in this unit

At the request of some users of the First Edition of this book, this Second Edition includes lists of new words at the end of each unit of the Teacher's Book.

The lists are not exhaustive, as it is assumed that learners will already know many of the words in the units. The lists include about 60 words and expressions that are not included in the five-language Glossary at the end of the Student's Book as they are very similar and instantly recognizable in French, German, Italian and Spanish.

agriculture	infrastructure
business	labour
company	manufacturing
consumer	primary sector
economic	product
economy	raw materials
employment	secondary sector
goods	tertiary sector
industry	unemployment

Unit 2 | Management

Management is important. The success or failure of business organizations, government institutions and public sector services, voluntary and non-profit organizations, sports teams, and so on, often depends on the quality of their management. This unit includes a discussion of the qualities required by managers, a definition of management, consideration of the role of meetings in management, a critical view of the management of one large American multinational company, and an interview with the manager of a British department store, who discusses his job.

A possible warm-up activity, before the discussion on the qualities required by managers and the definition of management, would simply be to discuss the cartoon. What's the joke? We can assume that Mr Farvis runs this company (his name is on the door). What can we say about his managerial skills, or his apparent lack of them?

Another possible warm-up activity (for classes that can be expected to know the answer) would be to ask learners to discuss in pairs for two minutes what exactly managers *do*, hoping to elicit vague notions (though probably without the correct vocabulary) concerning organizing, setting objectives, allocating tasks and resources, communicating, motivating, and so on.

1 Management – an art or a science?

1a Discussion

ANSWERS

1 The answer is probably that management is a mixture of innate qualities and learnable skills and techniques.

2 A personal choice of qualities: D, F, H and J. I also quite like K. If you like the sound of derisive laughter ringing round the classroom, tell any learners who choose L that they should consider becoming a teacher!

3 There are clearly no definitive answers as to which of these skills can be acquired.

An additional question Give some examples of famous managers. Whose career would you most like to emulate?

1b Reading

Peter Drucker, the (Austrian-born) American management professor and consultant, is the author of many books about business. The text paraphrases the extended definition of management he gives in one of his management textbooks.

Vocabulary note Many learners are unfamiliar with the plural of crisis, namely *crises* (in the penultimate paragraph). Also: thesis – theses, hypothesis – hypotheses, and their pronunciation.
    Outstanding, in the last line, here meaning exceptionally good, also has another meaning, as in an outstanding (or overdue) balance, etc.

ANSWERS

Drucker's first point (setting objectives and developing strategies) presumably requires qualities J, H, E and A (not necessarily in that order). The second point (organizing) presumably also requires H, E and J. The third point (motivation and communication) embraces F, D, I and probably C. The fourth point (measuring performance) probably requires H and E. The fifth point (developing people) might require H, F, D and J. But all this is clearly open to discussion.

1c Vocabulary

> **ANSWERS**
>
> 1 resources   2 manageable   3 setting, communicate   4 supervise, performance
> 5 achieved   6 board of directors
> 7 innovations

1d Vocabulary

> **ANSWERS**
>
> Common collocations include: allocate resources (or people), communicate information or decisions, develop strategies (or people or subordinates), make decisions, measure performance, motivate people, perform jobs, set objectives, and supervise subordinates.

1e Writing

These memos circulated for years in e-mails of lists of stupid sayings. You may well have received similar lists of stupid things said by lawyers, defendants, politicians, people making insurance claims, etc. They are apparently genuine (with the one about security cards coming from Microsoft). Your students may manage to do better (or worse). This is not a particularly serious exercise.

2 Meetings

Drucker obviously believes that work is largely something that is done individually, and that meetings are not 'work', but merely preparation for it, or consolidation after it.

2a Reading

Robert Cringely's history of the personal computer industry is very informative, in places very critical, and also very funny. In this extract, he is extremely negative about IBM, saying that they put much too much effort into management and worrying about the possibility of making bad decisions, and not enough into producing good, competitively-priced products.

2b Comprehension

> **POSSIBLE ANSWERS**
>
> 1 It seems as if the people who work for IBM are more interested in being regarded as a manager than as a computer designer or technician.
> 2 IBM's corporate culture seems to place more emphasis on management than on developing and selling the company's products.
> 3 IBM's managers don't actually do the work of designing and writing software themselves, but organize and supervise the people who do it.
> 4 IBM products are rarely as good or as cheap as similar products made by their competitors.
> 5 There is an extensive hierarchy and a system of checks and controls which ensures that bad decisions are generally avoided (but good decisions also take a very long time to make).
> 6 The slowness of IBM's decision-making process (and the consequent lack of competitiveness of their products) will eventually destroy the company.

2c Vocabulary

> **ANSWERS**
>
> 1 apparently   2 software   3 effort
> 4 hardware   5 trainees   6 expertise
> 7 layers   8 verify   9 amended
> 10 downfall

3 The retail sector

The unit finishes with the first of three extracts from an interview with the manager of a Marks & Spencer store. (The others are in Units 4 and 10.) M&S, as many people call them in Britain, sell clothes, household goods, and food.

3a Listening 🔊

Throughout this course, even where the instructions to the learners do not specify it, it will almost certainly be necessary to play each part of each recording at least twice.

> ### TAPESCRIPT
>
> *Steve Moody* So, as the store manager in Cambridge, which is probably the fortieth largest of the 280 stores we have got, I am responsible for the day-to-day running of the store. All the product is delivered to me in predescribed quantities, and obviously I'm responsible for displaying that merchandise to its best advantages, obviously I'm responsible for employing the staff to actually sell that merchandise, and organizing the day-to-day logistics of the operation. Much more running stores is about the day-to-day operation, and ensuring that that's safe, and obviously because of the two hundred people that we would normally have working here it's ensuring that they are well trained, that they are well motivated, and that the environment they work in is a pleasant one, that they are treated with respect, and that they are committed to the company's principles.
>
> *English for Business Studies Second Edition*
> © Cambridge University Press 2002

> ### ANSWERS
>
> Steve Moody says that he is responsible for the following tasks:
>
> 2 displaying the merchandise
> 3 employing the sales staff
> 4 ensuring the safety of staff and customers
> 6 getting commitment from the staff
> 8 maintaining a pleasant working environment
> 9 motivating staff
> 10 organizing the day-to-day logistics
> 14 supervising the day-to-day running of the store
> 15 training staff

Vocabulary note Steve Moody talks about the 'day-to-day running of the store', and 'running stores' appears in the question. Some learners may be unfamiliar with this synonym for managing.

3b Listening 🔊

> ### TAPESCRIPT
>
> *Interviewer* How much freedom do those people have within their jobs to make decisions themselves? How much delegation is there of responsibility down the chain?
>
> *Steve Moody* We would, as a business, like to encourage as much accountability and delegation as possible. Of course that does depend on the abilities of the individuals, the environment in which you're working, and the time of year. With 282 stores we have a corporate appearance in the United Kingdom's high streets. It is quite important that when customers come into Marks & Spencer's Cambridge they get the same appearance and type of looking store and the same level of service that they would expect if they went into Marks & Spencer's Edinburgh in Scotland, for example, and it's very important that we have a corporate statement that customers understand. So, there are obviously parameters and disciplines that,

you know, not only the staff but supervision and management would follow. Within that, in terms of development and training, training is obviously an investment for all staff. If staff are trained to do their job well and they understand it, they will feel confident in what they're doing, that in turn will give a better service to the customers, obviously from Marks & Spencer's point of view it could well lead to increased sales.

English for Business Studies Second Edition
© Cambridge University Press 2002

ANSWERS

1 Although Marks & Spencer 'would like to encourage as much accountability and delegation as possible', they have a corporate appearance for all their stores, in all of which customers should get the same level of service. This limits the freedom of individual managers to change the stores: there are 'parameters and disciplines that not only the staff but supervision and management would follow'.

2 Instead, they concentrate on staff development and training.

3c Listening 🔊

TAPESCRIPT

Interviewer Do you have meetings for members of staff where they can express views about what's going on in the store?

Steve Moody We have a series of meetings, management and supervisory every week, we have something which Marks & Spencer's call a focus group, which is members of staff who get together regularly from all areas of the store, so from the food section and perhaps the menswear section, from the office who do the stock and accounting, and indeed the warehouse where people receive goods. They have meetings, they discuss issues, they discuss problems that they feel are going on in the store. They also discuss suggestions of how they can improve that we run the store, and they discuss that amongst themselves first. They will then have a meeting with members of management and obviously myself, and we will discuss those issues and work together to try and provide solutions. However, Marks & Spencer's philosophy, I suppose, is that meetings should not be a substitute for day-to-day communication and therefore if problems do arise in terms of the operation, or an individual has got a problem in their working environment, or indeed their immediate line manager, or indeed if they have a problem outside, which might be domestic, or with their family, we would like to discuss that as it arises and would like to encourage a policy that they will come and talk to their supervisor or their manager, to see what we can do to solve the problem.

English for Business Studies Second Edition
© Cambridge University Press 2002

ANSWERS

1 A focus group.

2 Members of staff from all areas of the store (e.g. the food section, the menswear section, the stock and accounting office, the warehouse, and so on).

3 Staff can discuss problems in the store, and make suggestions for improvements. After this, they will meet with members of management to discuss those issues and try to provide solutions.

4 Individuals' problems with their work or their line manager, or even family problems.

5 Individuals are encouraged to discuss such problems with their supervisor or manager.

3d Discussion

Some learners may decide that they have the necessary abilities to become a manager or even a top manager; others may envisage more specialized careers in a particular function such as marketing, finance, computing, accounting, and so on, which will not involve managing and coordinating a large number of people and operations.

New words in this unit

allocate	merchandise
banker	motivate
board of directors	objective
chairman	organization
competitive	pay
customer	performance
director	promotion
distributor	resources
function	software
hardware	staff
innovation	strategy
investor	subordinate
logistics	supervise
manageable	supplier
management	tactics
manager	team
measure	top manager
meeting	trainee

Unit 3 | Company structure

One of the most important tasks for the management of any organization employing more than a few people is to determine its organizational structure, and to change this when and where necessary. This unit contains a text which outlines the most common organizational systems, an exercise which focuses on the potential conflicts among the different departments of a manufacturing organization, an example of an organization chart, and an extract from a talk by Jared Diamond concerning the best way to organize a business.

1 How are companies organized?

1a Discussion

This discussion activity follows on naturally from activity **3d** in the previous unit, about managing companies or having more limited responsibilities in a particular department.

1b Vocabulary

> **ANSWERS**
>
> | 1 C | 2 E | 3 B | 4 A | 5 F |
> |-----|-----|-----|-----|-----|
> | 6 G | 7 D | | | |

1c Reading

The text summarizes the most common ways in which companies and other organizations are structured, and mentions the people usually credited with inventing functional organization and decentralization. It mentions the more recent development of matrix management, and a well-known objection to it.

If you think that the learners may know the answers, the text can also be prepared orally by way of questions such as the following (each of which presupposes an answer to the previous one):

- How are most organizations structured?
- Yet most companies are too large to be organized as a single hierarchy. The hierarchy is usually divided up. In what way?
- What are the obvious disadvantages of functional structure?
- (*Discuss briefly in pairs*) Give some examples of standard conflicts in companies between departments with different objectives.
- Are there any other ways of organizing companies that might solve these problems?

> **ANSWERS**
>
> The diagrams are:
> A functional structure
> B matrix structure
> C line structure
> D staff position

Vocabulary notes In colloquial English we use the word *boss* rather than *superior*. We generally do *not* use the word *chief* (except in job titles, e.g. Chief Financial Officer).

Most companies have a *human resources* or *personnel* department; some American companies use the term *staff* department. *Staff* is a collective word for all the workers or employees of an organization. Staff in this sense is not the same as a 'staff position'.

1d Comprehension

ANSWER

The only adequate summary is the second. The first stresses the disadvantages of hierarchies much more strongly than the text, and disregards the criticisms of matrix management and decentralization. The third is simply misleading: matrix management and teams are designed to facilitate communication among functional departments rather than among autonomous divisions.

1e Discussion

ANSWERS

1, 4 and 11 would logically satisfy production managers, although 11 should also satisfy other departments.

2, 3, 6, 7 and 9 would logically be the demands of marketing managers.

5, 8, 10 and 12 would logically keep finance managers happy.

Note This exercise might be difficult for less advanced classes as it includes a number of words that are not defined here or practised elsewhere in the unit. Words which recur and are defined in later units (e.g. capacity, sales force, commission, features, market share, credit facilities, inventory, retained earnings) are *not* included in the vocabulary list at the end of the unit.

1f Describing company structure

Here is a short description of the organization chart illustrated.

The Chief Executive Officer reports to the President and the Board of Directors. The company is divided into five major departments: Production, Marketing, Finance, Research & Development, and Human Resources. The Marketing Department is subdivided into Market Research, Sales, and Advertising & Promotions. The Finance Department contains both Financial Management and Accounting. Sales consists of two sections, the Northern and Southern Regions, whose heads report to the Sales Manager, who is accountable to the Marketing Manager.

2 Competition and communication

2a Vocabulary

ANSWERS

1 C   2 F   3 E   4 A   5 G   6 B   7 D

2b Listening 🔊

TAPESCRIPT

Jared Diamond I've received a lot of correspondence from economists and business people, who pointed out to me possible parallels between the histories of entire human societies and histories of smaller groups. This correspondence from economists and business people has to do with the following big question: what is the best way to organize human groups and human organizations and businesses so as to maximize productivity, creativity, innovation, and wealth? Should your collection of people be organized into a single group, or broken off into a number of groups, or broken off into a lot of groups? Should you maintain open communication between your groups, or erect walls between them, with groups working more secretly?

How can you account for the fact that Microsoft has been so successful recently, and that IBM, which was formerly successful, fell behind but then drastically changed its organization over the last four years and improved its success? How can we explain the different successes of what we call different industrial belts? When I was a boy growing up in Boston, Route 128, the industrial belt around Boston, led the industrial world in scientific creativity and imagination. But Route 128 has fallen behind, and now Silicon Valley is the centre of innovation. And the relations of businesses to each other in Silicon Valley and Route 128 are very different, possibly resulting in those different outcomes.

I've spent a lot of time talking with people from Silicon Valley and some from Route 128, and they tell me that the corporate ethos in these two industrial belts is quite different. Silicon Valley consists of lots of companies that are fiercely competitive with each other, but nevertheless there's a lot of collaboration, and despite the competition there is a free flow of ideas and a free flow of people and a free flow of information between these companies that compete with each other. In contrast, I'm told that the businesses of Route 128 are much more secretive, and insulated from each other.

Or again, what about the contrast between Microsoft and IBM? Microsoft has lots of units, with free communication between units, and each of those units may have five to ten people working in them, but the units are not micro-managed, they are allowed a great deal of freedom in pursuing their own ideas. That unusual organization at Microsoft, broken up into a lot of semi-independent units competing within the same company, contrasts with the organization at IBM, which until four years ago had much more insulated groups. A month ago, I met someone who is on the board of directors of IBM, and that person told me, what you say about IBM was quite true until four years ago: IBM did have this secretive organization which resulted in IBM's loss of competitive ability, but then IBM acquired a new CEO who changed things drastically, and IBM now has a more Microsoft-like organization, and you can see it, I'm told, in the improvement in IBM's innovativeness.

So what this suggests is that we can extract from human history a couple of principles. First, the principle that really isolated groups are at a disadvantage, because most groups get most of their ideas and innovations from the outside. Second, I also derive the principle of intermediate fragmentation: you don't want excessive unity and you don't want excessive fragmentation; instead, you want your human society or business to be broken up into a number of groups which compete with each other but which also maintain relatively free communication with each other. And those I see as the overall principles of how to organize a business and get rich.

English for Business Studies Second Edition
© Cambridge University Press 2002

(This recording is not of Jared Diamond himself, but was read by an actor from a transcript of Professor Diamond's lecture.)

ANSWERS

1 1 A **2** B **3** D **4** D **5** B **6** C **7** A **8** C
2 g b c h i e k f d j a

Isolated companies or groups are at a disadvantage, because most groups of people get most of their ideas and innovations from the outside. So in order to maximize productivity, creativity, innovation, and wealth, you should break up your business into a number of groups which compete but also communicate with each other quite freely. You should also exchange ideas and information with other companies, and regularly engage staff who have worked for your competitors.

At the time of writing, the full transcript of Professor Diamond's talk is available at: http://www.edge.org/3rd_culture/diamond_rich/rich/_p1.html

3 Big and small companies

3a Discussion

> ### ANSWERS
>
> Advantages of working in a small company: 2, 3, 4, 7, 9, 11, 13
>
> Advantages of working in a big company: 1, 5, 6, 7, 8 (?), 10, 12, 14
>
> Some of these answers are open to discussion. For example, number 8: some people might argue that you have a better possibility of realizing your potential in a small company in which you are required to take on a number of different tasks.

3b Writing

This could be a homework activity. Learners should be discouraged from merely completing the paragraph given as an example.

There are further exercises on conjunctions and connectors in Units 19 and 27. The precise differences among words on the same line in the box (e.g. as, because and since) are difficult to demonstrate or explain. The use of these words is one of the things you could draw attention to in any supplementary texts you use in class.

New words in this unit

autonomous	insulated
boss	isolated
chain of command	level
Chief Executive Officer (CEO)	line authority
	Managing Director
collaboration	marketing
competitor	output
corporate ethos	personnel
decentralization	position
department	President
division	production
downsizing	productivity
downturn	reorganization
finance	report to
fragmentation	responsibility
functional organization	salary
	sales
hierarchy	subsidiary
input	wealth

Unit 4 | Work and motivation

As well as setting and communicating objectives, developing strategies, and allocating resources, managers have to motivate the staff who report to them. These will often include people with interesting, responsible and fulfilling jobs, as well as others with less interesting and highly repetitive tasks. This unit includes a discussion on whether it should be assumed that people like work and responsibility, or whether they need to be forced to work; a discussion about the kind of things that might motivate, or at least satisfy, employees; and an interview with a department store manager, who describes how he attempts to motivate his employees.

A possible warm-up would be to ask the learners to discuss briefly in pairs what is the worst possible long-term job they could imagine doing, one in which it would be almost impossible to motivate them, and why. (Someone will probably say 'Business English teacher', but of course we approve of humour in the classroom, don't we?!)

1 Work and responsibility

1a Vocabulary

> **ANSWERS**
>
> | 1 A | 2 B | 3 B | 4 C | 5 C |
> |-----|-----|-----|-----|------|
> | 6 B | 7 A | 8 B | 9 C | 10 B |

1b Discussion

As always, to be discussed in pairs. There are no 'right' answers, but these statements naturally fall into two groups, reflecting two opposing views of human nature, as will be seen in the text that follows.

1c Reading

> **ANSWERS**
>
> | 1 X | 2 Y | 3 X | 4 X | 5 Y | 6 X |
> |-----|-----|-----|-----|-----|-----|
> | 7 Y | 8 Y | | | | |

Abraham Maslow, mentioned here, is of course more famous for his own theory of motivation, and his pyramid of needs, with which most business learners are familiar. The Student's Book, I am pleased to say, is one of the very few books about business that does *not* mention this theory!

1d Summarizing

Learners can be asked to complete these sentences either orally (working in pairs), or in writing (alone or working in pairs).

> **TYPICAL ANSWERS**
>
> 1 According to Theory X, employers have to threaten workers because the threat of losing their jobs often makes people work better.
>
> 2 According to Theory Y, employers should give their workers responsibilities because a responsible job is necessary to people's psychological well-being.
>
> 3 Maslow criticized Theory Y because there are people who are unable to take on responsibility and self-discipline.
>
> 4 Maslow argued that even though they might want to be given responsibilities at work, people also require the security that comes from routines and from being given instructions.

1e Discussion

Learners' answers will almost certainly differ here. This task relates to the text in **1g**, which summarizes Herzberg's well-known argument that many of the items listed here (including good pay and good working conditions) merely *satisfy* but do not *motivate* workers.

1f Writing

This is probably a task to be set for homework.

1g Reading

According to Herzberg, good conditions merely *satisfy* workers, but do not *motivate* them; motivation can only come from interesting work, responsibility, and so on.

1h Summarizing

TYPICAL ANSWERS

1 Herzberg suggested that good labour relations and working conditions will only satisfy people – or more importantly, *dissatisfy* them if they do not exist – but not motivate them.

2 According to Herzberg, the kind of things that motivate people are challenging or interesting jobs, recognition, responsibility, the chance of promotion, and so on.

3 The problem with saying that only challenging, interesting and responsible jobs are motivating is that there are and always will be people in jobs that are *not* challenging, interesting and responsible, and managers have to try to motivate these people.

4 Ways of motivating people in unskilled jobs include giving them responsibilities as part of a team, giving them more than one activity to do during the day, and encouraging them to believe in corporate values.

5 The problem with trying to motivate workers by the belief that their company is the best is that it is unlikely to succeed if it is not true, and most companies are evidently not the best.

2 Motivating staff

2a Listening 🔊

This is a second extract from the interview with the manager of the Marks & Spencer store who featured in Unit 2.

TAPESCRIPT

Steve Moody In terms of keeping people motivated, the first thing is obviously ensuring that they are paid a decent salary and that they work in a pleasant environment. Beyond that, that they understand what is expected of them and that when they do do their job and they do carry out tasks, that what they do is actually appreciated by their line manager and indeed the people that they work with. They are not asked to do the same thing over and over again, yeah, without being told why they're being asked to do it.

Interviewer How important is a variety of tasks in motivating people? I mean, you wouldn't have somebody just working on the till the whole time, which I imagine is really hard work.

Steve Moody I think again it depends on the individual's abilities and the individual needs. We have people who work for us who actually like being on the till, all the time, because what they actually love, more than most, is the interface with the customers. They also, of course, become highly skilled, highly specialized, and highly efficient on the till, and if they like doing that and it actually suits us from an operational point of view, we would not discourage anybody from doing that. Equally, we've got members of staff who don't particularly like going on the till, but like filling up and doing stock orders and doing specific jobs that other people don't like doing, so it is tailoring individuals' needs and abilities to the operational needs of the store. Obviously you would not want to reduce flexibility by only having a certain number of people who will only go on the till, or only fill up the counters, you have to have flexibility of people who like to do both, and many staff like to do all sorts of things. They like to do everything they possibly can, and the more varied things they can get involved in, the more interested they get.

English for Business Studies Second Edition
© Cambridge University Press 2002

ANSWERS

1 Steve Moody says something similar to A, B and C. (A: he says a decent salary; B: he says a pleasant environment; C: he says they understand what is expected of them.) D and E are *not* what he says: he says that people must *be appreciated by* their line superior and their colleagues, and that people must not be asked to do the same thing again and again *without knowing why* they're being asked to do it.

2 Because they like the human contact (what he calls 'the interface') with customers.

3 They become highly skilled, specialized and efficient at this task.

4 Filling up the counters and doing stock orders.

5 Fitting, matching.

6 Because it gives them flexibility.

Note Some learners may erroneously suppose that 'tailor' has some relation to 'Taylorism', or the 'scientific management' associated with Frederick Taylor, which involved the strict division of labour, and so on. In fact, Moody is saying the opposite, and considering the worker as well as the task.

2b Listening 🔊

TAPESCRIPT

Interviewer M&S has a very good reputation for job security and looking after its staff, with things like good perks, good canteen, that sort of thing. Do those things actually motivate people, in their work, the fact that they're secure and well looked after, do you think?

Steve Moody I think it is, it is very important. When people have been working on the sales floor, and they may have been in from eight o'clock in the morning or seven o'clock in the morning, and they can come off the sales floor and they can go to the staff restaurant and obviously they can have tea, coffee, or a drink provided free of charge, and can then buy at very reduced rates a full cooked breakfast, if they want one, or a roll and cheese, in a pleasant environment, in a hygienic environment, food of the highest quality, there's areas where they can rest and read papers, or play pool or something, yeah, that is very important because they need a break from customers. At busy times, they need to get away from it, they need to be able to relax. In terms of all the health screening programmes we've got, that is very important, when people know that they will be having medicals, and the staff discount is another thing – obviously there's an amount of merchandise that they will buy which they will be able to buy at discounted rates. Christmas bonus, which I suppose for Marks & Spencer's, you know, we give all our general staff a 10% of their salary bonus at Christmas which is guaranteed, and the motivational effect of that, actually, at the busiest time of the year when they're under the most pressure and working hard, is fantastic and, you know, to see their faces as you hand them the envelope with 10% of their salary in it... I believe the environment that you work in, the quality of the people that you work with, the way you are treated, with respect and dignity, and the fact that your views are listened to, even if they're not always carried out they are listened to, and you feel you are consulted, that makes people happy in their job, it makes them satisfied in their job, it makes them get up and come to work in the morning.

English for Business Studies Second Edition
© Cambridge University Press 2002

ANSWERS

1 ● There is a restaurant where staff can get free drinks and good, low-priced meals.
   ● There is a place where they can relax during their breaks, read newspapers, play pool, and so on.
   ● They have regular medical screenings.
   ● There is a staff discount on M&S merchandise.
   ● There is a Christmas bonus of 10% of the annual (not monthly) salary.
   ● Staff are treated with respect and dignity, and are listened to and consulted.
2 It motivates them to work hard during the busiest period of the year (and a period in which they also have extra expenses).

2c Discussion

ANSWER

Steve Moody insists that the Christmas bonus, for example, actually *motivates* staff, whereas Frederick Herzberg argued that good salaries and working conditions merely *satisfy*. But Moody's statement that there are people who like a routine, and others who prefer a variety of interesting tasks, coincides with Douglas McGregor's argument.

2d Case study: Motivation

POSSIBLE ANSWERS

Bus drivers probably want enough consecutive days off to compensate for working irregular hours. They might appreciate facilities at the bus depot where they could socialize with colleagues before or after work. Yet few bus companies are likely to offer facilities as costly as a gymnasium or tennis courts. Drivers would almost certainly appreciate a subsidized canteen. Early retirement might be a good way of retaining staff for a large part of their working life, and would almost certainly be popular.

Nurses certainly do not do their job for the money. They are probably motivated by seeing their patients get better, and probably appreciate working regularly with the same patients. Public hospitals are clearly not in a position to implement a profit-sharing programme, and it doesn't even sound very appropriate for a private hospital, any more than productivity bonuses. Most nurses would probably appreciate a shorter working week. They would probably also respond favourably to career training, and perhaps to a nursery and sports facilities.

Sales reps in general seem to be motivated by high commissions, or a productivity bonus. They probably already have a company car. If they spend most of their time travelling, they are unlikely to be interested in a canteen, sports facilities, or a redecorated office. Few sales reps seem to stay long enough with the same company to be affected by extra days' holiday for long service or early retirement. They would probably be motivated by the knowledge that the products they sell are in fact beneficial.

A manual printing worker who remained for a large part of his or her career in the same company might well appreciate every single motivational strategy suggested. In reality, they are unlikely to be offered many of these, least of all a higher salary or a company car.

I have absolutely no idea how you would motivate a shepherd!

2e Vocabulary

ANSWERS

1 producer   2 products   3 productive
4 production   5 unproductive
6 productivity   7 pro'duce   8 'produce

Vocabulary note Many learners will probably be unfamiliar with the uncountable noun *produce* (stressed on the first syllable), which is only used for agricultural items (dairy produce, fruit, vegetables, flowers, and so on).

See also the role play 'Extra Perks' in *Business Roles 2* by John Crowther-Alwyn (Cambridge University Press).

New words in this unit

administration	produce
benefits	productive
cash register	reward
employee	sick pay
employer	skilled
incentive	store
job security	task
labour relations	threat
labour union	till
motivation	unskilled
pension	wages
perks	working conditions

Unit 5 | Management and cultural diversity

Despite the growth of global brands, and some degree of convergence of consumer tastes and habits, there remain enormous cultural differences among different countries and continents. This clearly presents a dilemma to multinational corporations: should they attempt to export their management methods to all their subsidiaries, or should they adapt their methods to the local culture in each country or continent? This unit contains a text that gives specific examples of problems faced by multinational companies in different parts of the world, and a number of discussion activities about cultural attitudes. Discussion activity **1a** serves as a ready-made warm-up to the unit.

1 Cultural attitudes

1a Discussion

It is generally agreed that it is more efficient for multinational companies to adapt their methods to the local cultures in which their subsidiaries are situated.

1b Discussion

The issues raised here are discussed in the reading text which follows. The learners' answers will reveal whether they believe companies should be task- or person-centred, whether they are primarily individualist or collectivist, and whether they are what Trompenaars calls universalist or particularist. They can be invited to suggest in which parts of the world the opposing opinions are to be found – and they may well be wrong.

Question 1 perhaps boils down to whether people or the functions they occupy are the most important. Are people all replaceable, or does the quality or the success of a business depend on its staff? For example, what is more important in a business school: the syllabus (maths, accounting, management, marketing, finance, production, law, information systems, etc.) or the people who teach these subjects? If it's the former, what makes the difference between better and worse business schools?

Question 3 seems to be related to Adam Smith's account of the beneficial outcome of self-interest and the notion of the 'invisible hand', with which the learners may be familiar. Two well-known passages:

'It is not from the benevolence of the butcher, the brewer, or the baker, that we expect our dinner, but from their regard to their own interest.'

[The self-interested individual] 'neither intends to promote the publick interest, nor knows how much he is promoting it … he intends only his own gain, and he is in this, as in many other cases, led by an invisible hand to promote an end which was no part of his intention.'

Adam Smith, *An Inquiry into the Nature and Causes of the Wealth of Nations* [1776] (Oxford: Clarendon Press, 1976, pp. 26–7 and 456).

An additional question to the learners: why are they studying business? For their own purposes (to get a good or better job) or to make the world a better place by aiding other people?

Question 4 raises the issue of collective responsibility. Learners who have done military service might have experience of situations of collective responsibility or punishment. Other learners may have experience of (or anecdotes about) playing team sports.

In Trompenaars' data, as reported in *Riding the Waves of Culture*, answers to the first question (Is a company a system or a social group?) varied widely within continents, allowing few conclusions to be drawn.

Nearly all countries answered question 2 (Is an organization structure about authority or functions?) by choosing function rather than authority, with scores of between 80 and 100%. Denmark, South Africa and Malaysia, countries with somewhat different cultures, all scored 100%. Venezuela on 44% was the only country below 50%.

For question 3 (individual freedom versus taking care of other people), most countries were spread between 50 and 70% for individual freedom. The lowest percentages came from Nepal, Kuwait, Egypt, East Germany and France – again, a varied bunch. The USA and Canada had the top scores for individual freedom – 79%. At last a stereotype appears to be fulfilled!

For question 4 (individual versus group responsibility) most scores for individual responsibility were between 30 and 50%. Indonesia was the most collectivist, with only 13% choosing individual responsibility, and Russia the most individualist, at 68%.

For question 5 (the car and the pedestrian), most northern European countries, along with Canada and Australia, scored over 90% for thinking that a friend should *not* expect you to lie. The lowest score here was 26% for South Korea. Russia was on 42%, and Japan on 67%.

2 Managing multinationals

2b Reading

> **ANSWERS**
>
> According to the text, the illustrated managers would be: a) American; b) Italian; c) Latin, or specifically French; d) and e) Asian or Southern European or Latin American.

2c Comprehension

> **POSSIBLE ANSWERS**
>
> 1 'Glocalization' means operating all over the world while taking account of local cultural habits, beliefs and principles in each country or market.

2 Japanese companies have a policy of promotion by seniority, so a 50-year-old manager should automatically be granted much more status and respect than a 30-year-old one.

3 The Italian salesman did not want to earn more (i.e. show himself to be a better salesman) than his colleagues, or earn as much as his boss. The Singaporean and Indonesian managers did not approve of a system that might cause salesmen to encourage customers to buy products they didn't need.

4 Universalists believe that rules are extremely important, and distrust particularists because they break rules to help their friends, while particularists believe that personal relationships should take precedence, and distrust universalists because they won't even help a friend.

2d Vocabulary

> **ANSWERS**
>
> 1 rationality   2 intuition   3 status
> 4 seniority   5 (to be) offended   6 rewards
> 7 bonus   8 humiliation   9 to resign
> 10 ethically

3 You and your culture

3a Discussion: You and your influences

As with various other exercises in the Student's Book (e.g. Unit 2 1a, Unit 4 1e, Unit 15 2f, Unit 22 1a), you may feel that too much information is given here in question 1. If you would prefer your learners to suggest these possible influences themselves, rather than merely select from a list, do a version of this exercise with the students' books closed. There are clearly no 'right answers' here.

3b Discussion: Attitudes to work

Again, there are of course no 'right answers'.

3c Survey

Doing this as an out-of-class survey would make a change from classroom discussion activities. What percentage of positive or negative answers to any question would be statistically significant and reveal cultural attitudes is hard to say. The figure of 60% in the Student's Book was *not* arrived at scientifically.

3d Discussion: Corporate culture

This discussion, and the next one, would probably work better with mixed classes containing learners of different languages, nationalities and cultures. If you have a homogeneous class, you could try to get them to suggest which countries or cultures might have motivated some of these questions (e.g. Japanese culture has very strict conventions about making eye contact).

3e Discussion: Body language

Again, you could try to elicit from the learners which cultures find some of these forms of behaviour *unacceptable*. For example, blowing one's nose in public is considered impolite in many east Asian countries. However this book is *not* going to provide a compendium of hints for foreign business travellers!

3f Discussion: Going abroad

Learners who have travelled might have things to say here. I thought my own nervousness about buying tickets on public transport was a personal pathology, until I went to conferences and saw famous professors walking three miles to the venue because they were too frightened to get on buses and trams! 'Do you have to leave a tip in this country?' is also a standard topic of conversation at conferences.

3g Writing

Even learners who have not been abroad should be able to think of information and advice that would be useful to a foreigner spending several weeks in their country. In fact, perhaps the memo needn't be 'brief' at all!

> See also the role plays 'Flexible working time' in *Business Roles* and 'No Smoking' in *Business Roles 2* by John Crowther-Alwyn, and the simulation 'The barbecue' in *Decisionmaker* by David Evans (Cambridge University Press).

New words in this unit

bonus	multinational
collectivist	negotiate
global	pay-for-performance
globalization	sales representative
individualist	seniority
localization	status

Unit 6 | Recruitment

The first section of this unit considers the process by which companies and other organizations recruit new members of staff, and discusses which kind of information given on a *curriculum vitae* or *resume* might help a job applicant to be selected for an interview. The second section contains an interview with a highly placed woman manager who discusses the place of women in management.

As a warm-up, the content of **1a** and/or **1b** could be discussed before looking at the book. You could try to elicit some of the necessary vocabulary by asking what people do if they are looking for a job, or what companies do when they want to hire somebody.

1 Filling a vacancy

1a Vocabulary

ANSWERS

1 job vacancies	2 employment agencies	
3 apply	4 candidate	5 applicant
6 application	7 application form	
8 curriculum vitae (CV) or resume		
9 references	10 job description	
11 short-listed	12 interview	

Vocabulary note Although Americans often use the word *resume* (sometimes with acute accents on the *e*s) rather than *curriculum vitae*, it must not be forgotten that the verb *to resume* in English does *not* mean to summarize, but to begin again.

The plural of *curriculum vitae* is *curricula vitae*.

1b Discussion

It will be seen from the chart on page 34 that the order of D and E could easily be reversed (i.e. some companies prefer to interview candidates personally before asking for references about them). If someone has been in a particular job for several years, the only reference that is really useful is his or her current employer's reference, but companies do not usually ask for current employer's references for candidates who are unlikely to be given the job.

Obviously, an employer should not reject all the other candidates until the selected candidate has agreed to accept the job. (Other non-short-listed candidates could, of course, have been rejected at an earlier stage, simultaneously with D or E.)

An additional discussion question In many cases, the perfect candidate for a job would be the person filling the same function at a company's chief competitor. Is it (a) legal and (b) ethical to approach such a person and offer him or her the job?

(*Answer:* In many countries employers ask employees to sign a contract stating that if they leave the company they will not join certain named competitors for a certain period of time. If you sign such a contract it is legally binding, but no one can force you to sign such a contract (though companies can of course refuse to employ you if you do not).

Leaving a company and joining another (or setting up your own) and using privileged information is of course illegal (and presumably unethical!), but sometimes difficult to *prove*.)

1c Case study: Job applications

An additional question How long do you think the human resources department spends looking at each application?

(*Answer:* It depends on who you talk to, but I have heard HR people say that on average, for junior jobs, they do not spend more than a minute per CV.)

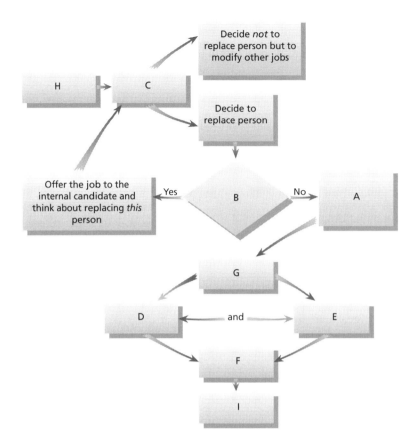

POSSIBLE ANSWERS

Questionnaire research of my own among leading employers of business graduates in continental Europe revealed the following information:

What employers like most is professional experience. Relevant experience is, of course, the most desirable, but not everyone has the possibility to do traineeships in companies. Failing that, work experience of any kind is a definite advantage. Even if you have only spent three weeks during a summer holiday filling the shelves in a supermarket it *is* work experience, and demonstrates that you can get up and go to work at 8 o'clock every day for three weeks, hence extract 4. Some students may object to the way extract 4 is written, and suggest writing 'stock management' instead of 'shelf filling'; I am unconvinced.

Travel, we say, broadens the mind, but if you've only ever travelled and never had a holiday job it doesn't look good. Extract 5 is supposed to be a parody, but there seems to be one student per class who selects it as the best! American culture seems to require more self-confidence than in much of Europe or Asia, but there remains a distinction between self-confidence and arrogance. 'Your company would have a great deal to gain from employing me' is way over the top.

Languages are usually an advantage for international business, although it depends on the job and the country. Swiss employers put this in second place, after work experience, and this is probably true of many countries. Lively students might well object to the way in which extract 2 is written. Indeed, they might object to the way *all* the paragraphs in this exercise are written.

Many companies are suspicious of people who seem only to have studied, and prefer people with a wide range of experience and interests to those with brilliant exam results but nothing else. But it depends on the job: high finance and R&D might require more evidence of brains than, say, jobs in selling (though this, too, is a subject for discussion). Students are very often prejudiced against those who get very high exam results, and may scoff at extract 7. If so, ask them how they feel about using a doctor, dentist, lawyer, architect or engineer who may have passed his or her degree with a mark of only 60% – i.e. getting 40% wrong!

Many employers expect to find a correlation between the amount of time and effort devoted to study and exam results. Hence low marks should be justified by extra-curricular activities. For a job that involves working closely with other people, evidence of having been a successful team-member, as in extract 1, is generally an advantage. But being a successful individual performer, as in extract 8, also shows determination, self-discipline, and so on. Apart from sports and hobbies, work in student associations, etc., is usually well thought of.

Extract 3 is appalling. Modesty and self-deprecating humour might be admired in some countries (such as England), but are not what is called for in job applications. Americans and Germans, for example, would almost certainly regard the writer of extract 3 as a complete idiot. A hobby like collecting phone cards does *not* make one an ideal candidate for a job in a telecoms company. It often reveals a shy, ingoing person, which is not ideal for a job in sales, public relations, and so on. Students may have something to say about this – or at least be prepared, as with extract 7, to parade their prejudices!

An appealing photograph is seldom a disadvantage, but they are rarely included in job applications in the USA.

1d Curriculum vitae (GB) or Resume (US)

This is just one way of writing a CV. Many other styles, and actual examples, can be found by doing a web search for, e.g., 'sample resumes'.

You may want to ask your learners to write a CV – though if they are first year students without much in the way of qualifications or work experience, they may prefer to wait a couple of years.

2 Women in management

2a Discussion

These issues are covered in the interview with Gill Lewis that follows.

An additional discussion question Simply ask the learners to explain the joke in the first **cartoon**.

2b Listening 🔊

> ### TAPESCRIPT
>
> *Interviewer* Gill Lewis, could you say something about the role of women in senior management, because there don't seem to be too many…
>
> *Gill Lewis* This is a thing I feel quite powerfully about because it's not surprising that it's a question that's often raised, given that in Switzerland above all other countries it's extremely unusual for a woman to be doing a job at the level that I'm doing, and indeed in 1970-something I was Businesswoman of the Year in the United Kingdom and that's, I think I might have said last, you might have heard me say this before, it's rather like being Miss World 1931, you know, there was no competition. And during that period I was a great disappointment to the media because they said to me, well, what does it take to be a successful woman, and I used to say largely the same as to be a successful man.
>
> I'm very much against affirmative action programmes. I think they do harm. I don't see how you can change the habits of millennia, of the man playing the role of the hunter and gatherer, the woman playing the role of the mother and home provider, just overnight. You simply can't do it, and if you try to force it, you're going to do harm.
>
> I see young women coming through now who are perhaps the first generation that are going to be – liberated is an overused word – but who are going to have choice in terms of the childbearing thing, and whether they can

be freed from the normal constraints of childbearing, whether they… with everything that goes with it, with the fact that parents bear more equally now the responsibility of bringing up children, with the fact that employers are more and more realistic about the fact that if they have a competent woman they're going to have to make some allowances. I think the generation of young women who are coming through now not only are going to have greater opportunity, but are also better prepared, and the young men with whom they are being educated are better prepared to treat them as equals too. So I think the world is changing pretty fast, not too fast, and I think that a lot of the affirmative action programmes that people do actually cause positive harm, because they end up saying why is Miss or Mrs X in the job, the answer is because she's a woman. Miss or Mrs X should be in the job because she's competent.

Now, having said that, I guess on a purely personal level if I've got two candidates for a job that I'm seeking to fill who are of equal competence, I mean genuinely equal competence, and I had to make a decision between the two of them, I suppose in the interests of the cause, if you will, I might, I might choose the woman – but only a woman that I was sure was going to follow through. Because earlier in my career I have been from time to time quite disappointed by women that I have recruited.

English for Business Studies Second Edition
© Cambridge University Press 2002

ANSWERS

1 Because there *were* hardly any businesswomen at the time (so there was virtually no competition).

2 The media expected her to explain the secret of being a successful businesswoman, and she replied that it was no different from being a successful businessman.

3 The man is the hunter and gatherer (i.e. the food provider) while the woman is the mother and home provider.

4 Men are now more prepared to share the responsibility for bringing up children; employers are now aware that if they want to hire competent women they are going to have to make some allowances; and their fellow students are better prepared to treat them as equals.

5 To make allowances here means to accept that women have to be treated differently from men, i.e. given maternity leave, and perhaps occasional time off to look after their children in emergencies, and so on.

6 Where there are affirmative action programmes, people will automatically assume that a woman only got a particular job because she's a woman, not because she's competent.

The somewhat surreal hunter-gatherer **cartoon** fits in nicely with Gill Lewis's description of the traditional role of the male, and probably requires no discussion.

See also the simulation 'The write stuff' in *Decisionmaker* by David Evans (Cambridge University Press).

New words in this unit

applicant	headhunter
application	interview
application form	job description
apply	job vacancy
candidate	reference
curriculum vitae or	resume or résumé
CV	short-list
employment agency	

Unit 7 | Labour relations

This unit discusses labour relations or industrial relations, and the nature and function of labour unions or trade unions. It contains an interview with Denis MacShane, a British Member of Parliament who is favourable to unions, a short extract from Bill Bryson's book about Britain, *Notes From a Small Island*, about the power of the printers' union in the British newspaper industry in the 1980s, and a text about industrial relations and unions in different countries. Discussion task **1a** probably requires no warm-up, although in countries which have recently experienced major labour disputes, the learners' experience of strikes could be discussed first.

1 Labour unions

1a Discussion

Labour unions or trade unions are organizations that attempt to represent workers' interests. They negotiate with employers about the wages, working hours and working conditions of their members. They can defend members who have individual grievances. If dissatisfied, they can take 'industrial action' such as going on strike or operating a go-slow or a work-to-rule. During a strike they can picket their place of work and try to prevent other workers or delivery drivers entering the premises.

1b Vocabulary

ANSWERS

1 D	2 C	3 B	4 F	5 A	6 E

1c Listening 🔊

TAPESCRIPT

Interviewer Denis MacShane, what would you say are the functions of trade unions, or labour unions?

Denis MacShane Work is changing all the time, but at the heart of work lies the worker, and as firms get bigger they require many workers, they have to be managed, and unions are a necessary voice for the interests of those workers. It is curious to see that in the new countries that have been in the headlines in recent years, countries like South Korea, or Poland, or South Africa, trade unions have played an enormous dynamic political and economic role. Clearly some of the old attitudes and structures of trade unions in Europe or the United States have become somewhat out of date and they have to be reinvented, but in the end, as long as employees have needs that need to be represented, then I think they'll need trade unions, and a sensible government, and sensible employers, that want effective social peace, and want also a team-working and dynamic economy, should be encouraging trade unions. The form of trade unions is changing, perhaps the old class war attitude of trade unions is out of date, but again it is interesting to see that some of the most successful economies – I'm thinking of Germany, I'm thinking of Japan – there is a strong trade union presence, it's recognized by employers, it is accepted as a partner by government.

English for Business Studies Second Edition
© Cambridge University Press 2002

ANSWERS

1a) MacShane says that unions are a necessary voice for the interests and needs of workers, and that in many countries they have played an enormous dynamic political and economic role.

1b) MacShane says that governments and employers that want social peace, and a team-working and dynamic economy, should encourage the existence of trade unions.

2 1 voice   2 dynamic, role
3 employees, represented   4 Sensible, peace, team-working   5 employers, partner

3 By 'class war attitude', MacShane means the Marxist idea that employers (and share-holders) are the enemy of the working class, and therefore need to be confronted by organized labour whenever possible.

1d Reading

This extract is slightly shortened, with sentences omitted. Younger students who have grown up with computers may need to have compositing or type-setting explained to them. The extract from Bryson's book doesn't mention that the printers' union had been able to negotiate their staffing levels, salaries and bonus payments because they had the power to call a union meeting or go on strike for a couple of hours any evening and prevent the newspapers appearing, causing huge losses for the owners.

ANSWERS

1 Bryson shows that newspaper managements were not very efficient and that the printers' trade union had been able to negotiate ridiculously uneconomical conditions. They had excessively high staffing levels (so that *The Daily Telegraph* was actually paying 300 people who didn't even come in to work), high salaries (*plump* means fat, or in this case, high), and excessive bonus payments, so that they got paid

extra for setting pages with editors' marks on them, for setting foreign words, etc. They even got compensated for *not* setting the type for advertisements that were done elsewhere.

2 He means that the situation was so serious (for the newspapers, not for their printers) that to describe the situation as 'out of control' isn't nearly strong enough. The situation was so bad it could not continue.

3 The statement about senior printers being among the top two per cent of British earners is apparently true. I suspect that the bit about printers receiving special bonus payments for the white space at the ends of lines (i.e. where they did not have to set any type) is a humorous exaggeration. But I am not certain.

4 All the newspapers started using a computerized system that allowed them to create pages from articles typed by the journalists on their own computers, so that type-setting became unnecessary, and all the printers lost their jobs. There were huge demonstrations by trade unions and sympathisers outside the new printing works of *The Times* for several months in 1986, which is where the photograph on page 50 was taken.

2 Industrial relations

2a Discussion

Business students should have some awareness of labour relations and the influence of unions in their country, whether in Europe, Asia, Latin America, or elsewhere.

2b Reading

The text mentions the paradoxical situation in one country – France – where on the one hand, many people consider that the unions are too powerful, as there are frequent strikes in sectors such as public transport, while other people, including politicians and managers, regret that the unions are not powerful enough, or at least not representative enough, as in some disputes mediators find no one to negotiate with.

1 Bad communications; an adversarial (management versus workers) attitude; a lack of consultation; and unions defending uneconomic working practices.

2 Working conditions of many people getting much worse; the creation of many unskilled, casual, part-time jobs done by non-unionized workers.

3 If workers are not represented by a union, there is no one representing the workers for management to negotiate with before or during a dispute.

Vocabulary notes French, Italian, Spanish and Portuguese speakers should be reminded that, in English:

– *negotiate, negotiation, negotiable*, and so on, always have a *t* after the *o*, rather than a *c* or a *z* (although it is pronounced as /sh/).

– a *syndicate* means a group of companies working together for a special purpose (e.g. a banking syndicate raising capital for a large project), but *not* a labour union.

2c Vocabulary

1 manual workers   2 trade union
3 consult   4 adversary   5 uneconomic
6 tyranny   7 deregulation
8 the public sector   9 confrontational
10 conglomerate

2d Discussion

When Peter Drucker writes 'Management is and has to be a power', he means that management has a distinct role, which is quite simply *to manage* – to decide what the company is going to do, today and in the future, how it is going to allocate its resources, and so on – without unnecessary outside interference. But by saying that power without any restraint or control becomes tyranny, he implies that unions have a legitimate right to defend the interests of workers.

Regarding the final question, large companies sometimes receive fiscal advantages (such as reduced taxes) from governments if they open a factory and create jobs in an area with high unemployment. In these cases they perhaps should *not* be allowed to close the factory as soon as the subsidies end.

New words in this unit

adversary	picket
collective bargaining	slowdown
consult	strike
deregulation	trade union
go-slow	uneconomic
industrial action	working practices
manual worker	working-to-rule
partner	

Test 1 | Management

Part One: Vocabulary

Which of these terms are defined below?

allocate	job description	motivate	resources
application form	job security	multinational	salary
autonomy	line authority	negotiate	short list
board of directors	logistics	objectives	skilled
decentralization	manual labour	personal	strike
factory	manufacturing industry	personnel	subordinates
functional organization	matrix management	planning	supervise
headhunters	merchandise	promotion	tertiary sector

1 a group of applicants selected for an interview

2 a short account of what a job consists of; the work that a particular employee is expected to do

3 a system in which decision-making passes from the top to the bottom of a hierarchy, as in the army, for example

4 a way of dividing a company into separate departments, depending on the tasks they carry out

5 an organization system in which people have responsibility to both a task or project and to their department

6 an organization's staff or work force; the people it employs

7 an organized refusal to work by a group of employees, in the attempt to achieve better pay or working conditions, or to protest about something

8 employees under someone else's authority or control

9 freedom to determine one's own behaviour and actions

10 people who attempt to engage senior managers and executives for job vacancies by attracting them from other companies

11 raising someone to a higher grade job

12 the extent to which a job can be considered as permanent

13 the part of the economy including services, commerce, marketing, banking, communications, transport, health care, education, and so on

14 to assign or designate resources for a particular purpose

15 to give an incentive to someone, to encourage

16 to talk to others in order to solve a problem or to reach an agreement

English for Business Studies Second Edition
© Cambridge University Press 2002

Part Two: Speaking

Allocate each learner one of the following subjects, to speak about for *two minutes*, after ten minutes of preparation with the Student's Book and their course notes.

1 Why is the tertiary sector regularly growing in the industrialized countries?
2 What are the functions of senior managers?
3 What are the advantages and disadvantages of functional organization?
4 What are the two approaches to managing people that Douglas McGregor called 'Theory X' and 'Theory Y'?
5 How do companies usually fill vacant positions?
6 What do labour unions do?

Give each learner *one* of the following questions to speak about for *one to two minutes*, after only two minutes of preparation *without* their books or notes.

1 Do you think anyone can learn to become a manager, or do you need particular skills and talents?
2 Have you ever worked for a particular manager who inspired you? What was good about him or her?
3 Do you think that women managers, in general, have any natural advantages over men?
4 Would you prefer to spend most of your career working for large or small companies, and why?
5 What benefits, not including a high salary, would you like in a job?

Part Three: Composition

Possible composition titles:

1 Is the decline of manufacturing in the old 'industrialized countries' inevitable?
2 What makes a good top manager, and what does he or she *do* all day?
3 What are the strengths and weaknesses of the 'traditional' functional structure used by many large companies? How could the weaknesses be remedied?
4 What can managers do to motivate people who do not have, or do not want, responsibility at work?
5 To what extent should multinational companies take into account local cultural characteristics when organizing subsidiaries?
6 Are labour unions a necessary partner to management, and is the relationship necessarily conflictual?

ANSWERS

Part One: Vocabulary

1 short list   2 job description   3 line authority   4 functional organization
5 matrix management   6 personnel   7 strike   8 subordinates   9 autonomy
10 headhunters   11 promotion   12 job security   13 tertiary sector
14 allocate   15 motivate   16 negotiate

Unit 8 Production

For a manufacturing company, production is obviously one of the four key functions, along with human resources, marketing and finance. This book gives far less space to production than the other functions for the simple reason that relatively few business students end up working in production management, which is largely the province of engineers. This unit contains vocabulary exercises relating to production capacity and inventory decisions; a text about just-in-time production methods; and an interview with a manager of a specialist hi-fi manufacturer about the importance of quality. There is also a role play about a production problem and a possible product recall.

1 Production decisions

1a Discussion

The **cartoon** provides a good lead-in to the subject. The joke concerns many business students' reluctance to go into manufacturing, and the delusion that business simply consists of making money rather than providing goods and services. Thousands of American business students in the 1980s wanted to get jobs on Wall Street and make a lot of money by trading bonds and other financial instruments.

Americans also have a reputation for being very litigious – taking other people or organizations to court and demanding money on almost any excuse.

An additional question The cartoon dates from 1987. Is this significant? Do you think business students have changed since then?

(*Answer:* This cartoon was first published in November 1987, a month after a big stock market crash. It is widely argued that the financial excesses of the 1980s did not survive into the 1990s.)

Production and operations managers should presumably be interested in making products or providing services rather than simply making money. They usually need a lot of technical knowledge (about manufacturing processes) and mathematical abilities (which are not treated at all in this book). Even in these days of increasing automation, good human relations skills are also a clear advantage.

The objectives of the production department are usually to produce a specific product, on schedule, at minimum cost. But there may be other criteria, such as concentrating on quality and product reliability; producing the maximum possible volume of output; fully utilizing the plant or the work force; reducing lead time; generating the maximum return on assets; ensuring flexibility for product or volume changes, and so on. Some of these objectives are clearly incompatible, and most companies have to choose among price, quality, and flexibility. There is an elementary trade-off between low cost and quality, and another between low cost and the flexibility to customize products or to deliver in a very short lead time.

1b Vocabulary

> **ANSWERS**
>
> 1 subcontractor   2 component
> 3 outsourcing or contracting out   4 capacity
> 5 plant   6 location   7 inventory
> 8 lead time

Learners may make mistakes choosing which syllable to stress in some of these words (e.g. com'ponent, lo'cation and con'tracting are stressed on the second syllable, 'inventory is often reduced to three syllables with the 'o' being silent, and 'subcontractor is stressed on the prefix). There is a fairly extensive section on word stress in the Language reference section of the Student's Book (on page 181), which learners should be encouraged to consult on more than one occasion.

Vocabulary note *Location* in English, meaning place, is of course not the same as *location* in French, meaning rental.

1c Vocabulary

Note *Excess* in heading B has a negative connotation (unlike *spare* capacity which could be an advantage).

SUGGESTED ANSWERS

1 A and E	2 C	3 D	4 A and E
5 A and E	6 D	7 F	8 E
9 F	10 E	11 B	12 E	13 B
14 C and E	15 B and F		

The photo from Charlie Chaplin's film *Modern Times* (1936) might give rise to a discussion about changes in manufacturing industry in recent decades: the rise of technology, automation, robotics, and so on.

1d Reading

The subject of this text – just-in-time production – clearly relates to the previous exercise about capacity and inventory size. With learners who have followed a course in production management it will be possible to elicit much of the information contained in the text with questions such as:

- What is just-in-time production?
- Where did it originate?
- What are the obvious advantages and disadvantages?

Additional questions, to be asked either before or after reading the text, depending on the learners' knowledge, include:

- Is the JIT system used in your country?
- If not, do you think it could easily be introduced?

ANSWERS

1 component   2 subcontractor
3 inventory   4 outsourcing   5 location
6 plants   7 capacity   8 lead times

1e Comprehension

ANSWERS

1 True ('Each section of the production process makes the necessary quantity of the necessary units at the necessary time – which is when it is required by the next stage of the manufacturing process, or by distributors or customers.')

2 False (Ohno mentioned American retailing.)

3 False (Quite the contrary; it encourages them to produce exactly the amount required.)

4 True ('…if a single subcontractor fails to deliver a component on time, the whole production process is sabotaged.')

5 False (There is virtually no inventory.)

6 True ('…the Japanese industrial system relies on mutual trust and long-term relationships.')

7 True ('This avoids all the waiting and moving time involved in sending half-finished items from one department to another. […] JIT…should ensure that there is no waste…from idle workers waiting for parts.')

8 False ('The Japanese also prefer small, specialized production plants with a limited capacity. […] very small production runs are possible.')

9 True (This is not mentioned in the text, but follows logically from the concept of JIT, as business students should be able to understand. In fact it was one of my students who suggested this as a disadvantage of JIT since I wrote the first edition!)

2 Quality

2a Discussion

These questions should generate the adjectives or nouns often used in relation to quality: performance, appearance, reliability, durability, and so on.

POSSIBLE ANSWERS

1 ● Fast-food customers are usually looking for speed of service, relatively low prices, reasonable food, and consistency – an identical product in all a fast-food chain's outlets.

 ● A restaurant meal usually takes more time, but the service should not be too slow. The food is expected to be good, and possibly distinctive – not the same as in all other restaurants. The decor and atmosphere are important.

 ● A tennis club should have good facilities, a good atmosphere, and offer sufficient opportunities to play, i.e. not have too many members.

 ● A small car is probably a relatively cheap one (luxury cars tend to be big). It will not perform like an expensive sports car, but it should be reliable and durable. It may not have as many features as larger cars, but should still have a good appearance.

 ● A raincoat should keep you dry, i.e. be waterproof, but also last a reasonable length of time, and look good. Appearance is probably important. 'Serviceability' might also be important: can you just throw it in the washing machine, or does it have to be dry-cleaned?

 ● Hi-fi equipment should obviously reproduce sound with high fidelity, i.e. what comes out of the speakers should be exactly what is recorded on the CD, tape, etc. On expensive hi-fi equipment it is also possible to change the sound by boosting the bass, middle and treble frequencies, and so on. Hi-fi equipment should also be durable, i.e. it should last a number of years without needing to be repaired.

2 Examples of avoidable expenses relating to a lack of quality include: identifying the causes of defects, implementing corrective action, training or retraining personnel, redesigning a product or system, scrapping, reworking, repairing, servicing or replacing defective products, handling complaints, losing customers or their goodwill, and so on.

2b Listening 🔊

TAPESCRIPT

Alan Severn I'm Alan Severn, I'm the Quality Manager at Arcam, and my responsibilities are exactly that, for the quality of the product, the quality of the services, and the quality of all interfaces which involve the customer and our customers.

   The word 'quality' is a very easy one that slips off the tongue, it's quite easy to say but it means an awful lot of things. I have a department of three people, but in essence, everybody in the company works for me, because everybody works for the word 'quality'. Quality starts and must start at the conception of everything and go through every department within the company. You can't pack quality into a box at the end of the line. You have to implant it at the start of a process, and it knocks on through every process until it goes into a box, into your home, into your living room, and you switch it on and you're a happy person.

   The two aspects of quality are that we must reproduce, must, sorry, design to reproduce excellent hi-fi equipment, and that must be a design which has got quality built into it in terms of the performance of the product, but also must have the ability to be produced in volume. Er, now, that means the designers have to have restraints put on them, and that restraint means that they must work to quality standards to ensure that their designs are reproducible in volume. They must design for manufacture. Now that's one part of the quality aspect and that's where it starts within Arcam, the ability to have (a) a perfect design and (b) that the design is reproducible.

   They hand that information on to our manufacturing departments. Now the manufacturing departments have the same, erm, the same message, the same cause in life, to then, to make sure that the designs that are now designed for manufacture are designed, sorry, are manufactured, for production. Now that may sound a bit daft, but when you move in to the next stage you have to productionize the designs, you have to ensure that the things will go together every time on the line. And that's a function of design, it's a function of manufacture, that when two pieces of metal come together, that they go together every time, five hours a day, ten hours a day, 28 days in a month, etc., etc.

And to that end we have to then implant into our suppliers, and our manufacturing people, the quality standards which will achieve that aim, our goals. So, our message spreads then from our designers into our manufacturers and our subcontractors who make the metalwork, who make the printed circuit boards, who assemble the printed circuit boards, etc., etc.

Quality's a very well-worn word and in this business, certainly in Arcam's business, it is an ongoing activity within the company, and it's called TQM, Total Quality Management, that we improve our quality on a daily, weekly, monthly, yearly basis. So we never stop refining the process. Erm…we don't know when we're going to arrive there because we don't know what the ultimate quality is. I guess the ultimate quality is that we build a thousand units, we ship a thousand units, and we don't get any of them back, and they last for ten years. That I think is probably…you've arrived.

English for Business Studies Second Edition
© Cambridge University Press 2002

ANSWERS

1 Alan Severn says that he has three members of staff in his department, working directly for him, but it could also be said that everybody in the company works for him, because everybody in the company – in design, production, marketing, and so on – is concerned with quality.

2 The products must, obviously, include a high quality of sound reproduction (they must come as close as possible to perfect design), but it is also important that this design is reproducible, i.e. it must be possible to 'productionize' the design, to produce a large volume of equipment with this same quality.

3 Quality begins with the designers, who have to design manufacturable, high quality products. The designers' quality specifications are then explained to the suppliers of components.

4 By TQM, Alan Severn means the never-ending process of continuously improving and refining quality.

5 Although you can never know if you have achieved the ultimate level of quality, Alan Severn says that if the company builds and sells a thousand units, and none of them are returned as defective, and all of them last for ten years, he would accept this as a sign of perfect quality.

2c Role play

Groups of two or three learners can prepare each role for five to ten minutes, though only one person should take on the role in the meeting. (Role plays in which each participant insists on having 'an assistant' at his or her side tend to become chaotic.) This role play would be difficult to do with classes of fewer than seven learners, as all the roles are important.

The role of Managing Director, who chairs the meeting, should be given to a good speaker. This role is crucial, as is deciding in which order the other participants speak. The meeting should follow the instructions given in the Managing Director's role; if, for example, the Production Manager speaks first, the rest of the possible discussion is likely to be short-circuited.

The language of meetings is not included in this book, but is covered in detail in *English for Business Communication* by Simon Sweeney (Cambridge University Press).

These are the roles to be photocopied and given to the groups of learners:

ROLE 1

The Managing Director

You have to explain the situation to your colleagues, listen to their opinions, and decide on a plan of action. You are chairing the meeting. Therefore you decide who speaks, and in what order. You should prevent people speaking or interrupting without your permission. In order to respect status and hierarchy, you have decided to listen to the four company directors present at the meeting (the marketing director, financial director, human resources director, and the head of the legal department) first, followed by the managing director of the bottle supplier, and finally the production manager of the bottling plant.

English for Business Studies Second Edition
© Cambridge University Press 2002

ROLE 2

The Head of the Legal Department

You are alarmed by this news, and believe that all existing supplies of *Lift* must be recalled immediately – all over Europe and especially in the United States. The financial consequences of someone being injured or killed by a faulty product in the US could be catastrophic, as people there are occasionally awarded sums of many millions of dollars for even minor injuries. Consumers are encouraged to sue companies for ridiculous amounts of money by unscrupulous lawyers who work for free, but take 30% of any out-of-court settlement or damages awarded by a court. You think the cost of an international product recall is a price worth paying to avoid any potential legal difficulties.

English for Business Studies Second Edition
© Cambridge University Press 2002

ROLE 3

The Marketing Director

You think that the product must be recalled immediately. The risk of someone being hurt by broken glass in a bottle of *Lift* is too big to take. If someone is hurt, sales would drop anyway, and the whole company's image would suffer disastrously. Withdrawing all existing bottles of *Lift* from sale and destroying them would be expensive, but this is the only possible solution. In the long run, the company's image will improve if it is seen to take strong action here.

English for Business Studies Second Edition
© Cambridge University Press 2002

ROLE 4

The Financial Director

You are horrified by the cost of a product recall, when you don't know how widespread the problem is. On the other hand, if you do not withdraw the product and someone is hurt your company will receive terrible publicity and your sales and stock price will fall, reducing both your profits and your market value. You think the product should be withdrawn, but only if it can be shown that more than a dozen bottles are affected.

English for Business Studies Second Edition
© Cambridge University Press 2002

ROLE 5

The Human Resources Director

You do not have a strong opinion about whether bottles of *Lift* should be withdrawn from sale. What you want to know is whether the problem is due to empty bottles being supplied to your company with pieces of glass in them, or whether there was an accident or sabotage in the bottling plant. You suspect sabotage because you know that some of the workers at the bottling plant are angry as one of their colleagues was recently fired after being caught stealing some maintenance tools. You were opposed to this action, which was taken by the production manager at the plant. You warned him at the time that he risked a strike or sabotage or some such action by dissatisfied employees, but he refused to listen to you.

English for Business Studies Second Edition
© Cambridge University Press 2002

ROLE 6

The Managing Director of the bottle supplier

You are convinced that any glass found in bottles of *Lift* was put there in the bottling plant. You supply bottles to six different manufacturers, and your quality control is excellent. You have never had a case like this before, in 30 years of business. You are certain that this must be a case of sabotage in the *Lift* bottling facility. You do not have any clear opinion about whether the product should be withdrawn from sale, and are only determined to demonstrate that your company is not responsible. You want to know what labour relations are like at the bottling plant, and whether any of the workers might have any reason to want to sabotage the drink and damage the company.

English for Business Studies Second Edition
© Cambridge University Press 2002

ROLE 7

The Production Manager of the bottling plant

You do not think it possible for bottles to leave your factory with broken glass in them unless it was put there deliberately by workers. But this would be very difficult to do. You suspect that this may be the result of criminal activity by a small group of workers. You find it very surprising that people who find glass in a bottle simply return the drink to the place where they bought it without leaving their name and address. You suspect that this was the work of people who managed to sabotage a few bottles and who then took them to the shops in the north of England and Belgium. Both places are very easy to get to from London. If this is the case, there is no need to withdraw the drink from sale in nine different countries. You should not make an announcement to the media, but rather call in the police to investigate. You also think it is time to install an entirely automated production system which would prevent workers from being able to sabotage the product. It fact it would eliminate production workers entirely, which would be a good thing.

English for Business Studies Second Edition
© Cambridge University Press 2002

See also the role play 'Quality and personnel' in *Business Roles* by John Crowther-Alwyn (Cambridge University Press).

New words in this unit

assemble	opportunity cost
capacity	outsourcing or
component	contracting out
economies of scale	parts
equipment	plant
facilities	production run
inventory	quality
just-in-time	set-up
production	storage
lead time	subcontractor
location	supplies
operations	work in process

Unit 9 | Products

This is the first of four units on marketing. It contains a text defining products, brands, product lines, line-stretching, and so on; an interview with the director of a company that is planning to launch a new product all over the world; and a short case study concerning products sold by way of vending machines. Discussion task 1a, about successful brands and the learners' own brand loyalty, is a natural lead-in to this topic.

1 Product policy

1a Discussion

The 'products' illustrated include the singer Britney Spears, the golfer Tiger Woods, the Eiffel Tower, and a New York Yankees baseball cap.

Here is a possible discussion topic to start the lesson:

Perhaps the ultimate triumph of a brand is when its name enters the language. For example, a majority of English people talk about a *hoover* rather than a vacuum-cleaner, and use *hoover* as a verb (as in 'I'm just going to hoover the living room'). A lot of people say *kleenex* instead of paper tissue, and *sellotape* instead of sticky tape or adhesive tape. The ball-point pen was invented by a man called Biro, and lots of English people still talk about *biros*.

Are there any words like this in your language?

Products in the contrary situation, that people buy without even noticing the brand name, might include ball-point pens, pencils, erasers, pencil sharpeners, note paper, writing paper, envelopes, and so on, as well as matches, salt, sugar, flour and other cooking ingredients.

The reasons for brand loyalty can vary. Consumers may be satisfied with the quality and price of the brand, and so have no reason to change; they may consider a brand to be fashionable, and therefore desirable; they may be influenced by continuous advertising; or they simply have unwittingly acquired a habit, which saves them the time and effort necessary to make a choice whenever they go shopping.

1b Reading

POSSIBLE ANSWERS

1 What is a product?/The definition of a product
2 Brand names
3 Product lines and product mixes
4 Line-stretching and line-filling

1c Comprehension

POSSIBLE ANSWERS

1 Because this allows them to cover several market segments, leaves less space for competitors' products, and makes it more likely that brand-switchers will occasionally buy their products.
2 Because they usually include products that are reaching the end of their life cycle, and because consumer needs, market opportunities, and the company's possibilities are always evolving.
3 Overall company objectives, such as whether they are looking for a large market share, or market growth, or high profitability, and so on.
4 Stretching a line to the lower end of a market may damage a company's image for quality. Conversely, companies making cheap products might not convince the market that they can also make quality products.
5 Companies might fill their product lines in order to compete in niches previously occupied by competitors, or in order to use spare production capacity.

1d Vocabulary

2 Developing a new product

2a Discussion

The advantages of vending machines include:

- They can be installed almost anywhere.
- You don't have to pay sales staff, just someone to fill, clean and maintain the machine.
- They can function 24 hours a day, 365 (or 366) days a year.

The disadvantages include:

- They can be vandalized.
- If they are broken, the customer can lose his or her money.
- It must be possible to adjust prices on machines because of inflation and changes of coinage or currency.

An additional discussion question If, like many people, you only use vending machines when shops and stores are closed, do you agree with the laws regulating the opening hours of stores in your country? What are the reasons for such laws?

(*Answer:* To protect retail employees: to make sure that they are not obliged to work long, anti-social hours. In some countries, these laws apply to employees, but not to members of the family of the owner of a small business.)

2b Listening 🔊

TAPESCRIPT

Interviewer Jogishwar Singh, I recently read a newspaper article in which one of your business partners announced, 'We are going to invade the whole world with a revolutionary product that is going to be more popular than McDonalds.' Could you explain exactly what this product is?

Jogishwar Singh This product is crisp, hot, fresh french fries, which will be delivered by a vending machine. All that the customer has to do is choose the number of portions, one, two, three or four, pay the corresponding amount which he can see on the machine because the amount will vary according to the country, put the money in, wait 64 seconds for the first serving, and then eat the chips which will come out nicely in a very beautiful looking, striking container, a cup.

Interviewer So this machine can be installed in the street, as well as in restaurants, or cafés…

Jogishwar Singh Well, the idea is to install it in public places, you know, not so much inside restaurants, but, you know, anywhere where people gather you can install the machine: airports, railway stations, football stadiums, sports centres, service stations, cinema halls, anywhere, literally anywhere where people want a nice cup of french fries.

Interviewer And these fries are made from powdered, a powdered potato mixture?

Jogishwar Singh That is correct. They are made from dehydrated potato powder, to which we add certain ingredients, you know, which are subject, well, which are secret, which we keep to ourselves.

Interviewer So this is a vending machine; there are no plans to make a smaller version, to put in your kitchen?

Jogishwar Singh There is. We are, after the proper launching of the vending machine, the inventor is already working on what he calls a table-top machine, you know, which will be for kitchens or for kiosks or smaller places, yes.

Interviewer And could you talk perhaps about all the various stages that come between an inventor – this is an American inventor…

Jogishwar Singh Yes, Mr Richard Sorensen.

Interviewer …having the idea and then now your company launching this product?

Jogishwar Singh Well, the inventor had the idea and he did the first, I mean he developed obviously his ideas, he's been working on it for the last eight or nine years. He got into touch with people who subsequently became shareholders in the holding company Tégé, and he went through a series of at least five prototypes, each time modifying the design because, you know he found new, not really inventions, but new technical support to improve the functioning, to reduce the time of delivery, and the problem is basically financing, you see. It's extremely difficult for an individual to finance such a major project. So he was looking for partners. And we have put, you know, experts and engineers at his disposal. This is important because an inventor is not an industrial engineer, you know. He might be a brilliant inventor but he doesn't have much of an idea, well in this case of industrial production, and the economics of the whole project. So we surrounded him with very capable people who are costing us a fortune, and the machine will be manufactured by Zanussi, one of the two leading vending machine manufacturers in Europe and the world.

Interviewer So for you the technological advance is the machine, rather than the product, because powdered chips sounds quite revolutionary as well?

Jogishwar Singh That is correct. It's the machine; it's the time in which you can deliver the chips; it's the crispiness and the quality with which you can deliver the chips; and more than these things it's the consistency. You see, if we can manage to deliver the same product in 180 countries in the world, I think that's where the success of this project will lie.

Interviewer And you're aiming at 180 countries?

Jogishwar Singh Oh, yeah, yeah. Doubtlessly, certainly. Over… Not immediately, but I am sure we will see our vending machines with the same logo, the same colour scheme, whether you are in Bangladesh or Taiwan or the US or Europe or wherever, Africa, I mean, you know, it might take us some time getting to Rwanda but we will get there.

English for Business Studies Second Edition
© Cambridge University Press 2002

ANSWERS

1 C ('the idea is to install it in public places, you know, not so much inside restaurants, but, you know, anywhere where people gather')

2 C ('They are made from dehydrated potato powder, to which we add certain ingredients, you know, which are subject, well, which are secret, which we keep to ourselves')

3 A ('a table-top machine, you know, which will be for kitchens or for kiosks or smaller places')

4 B ('he found new, not really inventions, but new technical support to improve the functioning, to reduce the time of delivery')

5 C ('an inventor is not an industrial engineer, you know. He might be a brilliant inventor but he doesn't have much of an idea, well in this case of industrial production, and the economics of the whole project')

6 B ('more than these things it's the consistency. You see, if we can manage to deliver the same product in 180 countries in the world, I think that's where the success of this project will lie')

2c Vocabulary

> **ANSWERS**
>
> 1 portions   2 chips   3 striking
> 4 dehydrated   5 ingredients   6 kiosk
> 7 shareholders   8 fortune   9 consistency
> 10 logo

2d Discussion

The interview with Jogishwar Singh was recorded in 1995. The first Fresh Fries machines were installed later that year. Unfortunately, the machines did not work as well as hoped, and the fries tended to come out a bit soggy. Customers were disappointed and few vending machine operators were interested in taking on the machine. The share price, which in 1998 rose to over 200 Swiss francs when investors believed that the machine had great potential, fell to around 5 francs in 2001, and the company, which had used up 58 million Swiss francs worth of investors' money (including rights issues), was unable to raise any more capital, and the Fresh Fries concept was abandoned. Swiss financial journalists described the machine as a 'mirage' and the company's use of shareholders' capital as a 'con'. However, Tégé has been a quoted company in Switzerland since 1931 – beginning life as a funicular railway (!), and later moving into the property business, before taking on the Fresh Fries concept – and it was bought by a mobile phone retailer to gain quick access to the stock market.

2e Preparing a report

This is probably best done in groups of three. The groups can be given 15 or 20 minutes to make a first draft of their report, and then report back to the rest of the class. One group can be chosen to report on the current market situation; the other learners can be invited to agree or disagree. Then other groups can be asked to suggest new vending machine products, after which the class can give their opinions on the likelihood of success.

The final report could obviously be prepared as a **writing** exercise.

The content of the report will probably include much of what was said in discussion task **2a**. Many people only use vending machines when they have forgotten to buy something, or are hungry, but the shops and cafés are closed.

2f Discussion: M-commerce

At the time of writing (2001), it is being widely predicted that m-commerce or mobile commerce is going to expand rapidly and overtake e-commerce (electronic commerce, discussed in Unit 29), that within two years there will be more mobiles than personal computers linked to the internet, and that Visa and MasterCard will develop a way to put a credit or debit card function in a mobile phone, along with the SIM card.

If all this comes to pass before your learners do this unit, they may find this discussion a little out-of-date. On the other hand, the more m-commerce services that become available, the more they might be inspired to think of new ones, even if they only involve vending machines.

With classes that are keen on IT, you could probably do Unit 29 out of sequence (e.g. after this unit), as it does not require a knowledge of the vocabulary and concepts in the intervening units on marketing, finance and economics.

> See also the role plays 'Changing names' and 'New products' in *Business Roles* by John Crowther-Alwyn (Cambridge University Press).

New words in this unit

after-sales service	multi-brand strategy
brand	niche
brand name	product life cycle
brand-switcher	product line
credit facilities	product mix
delivery	product range
down-market	profitability
image	profitable
launch	prototype
line-filling	retailer
line-stretching	shelf
logo	up-market
market segment	vending machines
market share	warranty or guarantee

Unit 10 | Marketing

Marketing has long been considered one of the basic functions of business organizations. More recently, it has been argued that it is *the* central function, to which the other departments must all be subservient. This unit offers two definitions of marketing; a text which discusses the 'marketing concept' (as opposed to the previously prevalent 'selling concept'), market research, the marketing mix and industrial marketing; an interview with a department store manager who discusses a hypothetical marketing failure and the possible remedies; and a short case study about market research.

1 Defining marketing

A possible warm-up, before reading the definitions of marketing, would be to ask learners, perhaps in pairs, to suggest their own definitions. Learners who have not followed marketing courses are likely to propose a much more restricted definition than those found in marketing books, perhaps limiting it to market research surveys and advertising. Task **1a** will then introduce them to more comprehensive definitions.

1a Definition

> **ANSWERS**
>
> 1 identify   2 develop   3 persuade
> 4 modify   5 design   6 influence

Drucker's definition seems to be a little optimistic, and overlooks the existence of competition: a successful product will soon attract imitators or rivals onto the market. Even if you have an exceptional product that consumers want to buy, it is unlikely to be the only one on the market.

1b Vocabulary

> **ANSWERS**
>
> | 1 A | 2 I | 3 F | 4 H | 5 D |
> |-----|-----|-----|-----|-----|
> | 6 J | 7 E | 8 B | 9 C | 10 G |

Vocabulary note French, Italian and Spanish speakers often confuse the English words *channel*, *canal* and *chain*. In English, we talk about distribution channels and television channels and not chains or canals. Shops with lots of branches are known as chain stores or supermarket chains, but this is not the same as a distribution channel. A canal is an artificial waterway, while the narrow sea between England and France is – of course – called the English (not French) Channel!

1c Reading

The beginning of the text follows from the definitions in **1a** and **1b**. With learners who have followed marketing courses, some of the other notions in the text could be elicited by questions such as 'What is the marketing mix?' and 'What is industrial marketing?'

> **ANSWERS**
>
> Paragraph 1 – the selling and marketing concepts
> Paragraph 2 – identifying market opportunities
> Paragraph 3 – the importance of market research
> Paragraph 4 – the marketing mix
> Paragraph 5 – company-to-company marketing

1d Comprehension

ANSWER

The third summary is the most accurate and complete. The second summary fails to mention market research, and both the first and second contain errors. They both neglect the continued importance of selling, and the existence of competitors. They also wrongly suggest that market segmentation is the only way to find a market opportunity: some products are aimed at wholly new, unsegmented markets. The first summary wrongly states that marketers regularly *have to* change a product, its distribution, the way it is promoted, and its price. In fact they *may* change one or more of these elements as necessary. The second summary states that the marketing of industrial or producer goods is 'more important' than that of consumer goods, which is untrue.

Vocabulary note In English, unlike in French, *important* only means *significant* and not large or big.

1e Comprehension

ANSWER

C

2 The importance of market research

2a Listening 🔊

This short listening extract is not so much about marketing as a hypothetical marketing failure, which Steve Moody mentions while explaining the respective roles of head office and the individual stores.

An additional discussion question What percentage of new products do you think fail?

(*Answer: Most* new products fail, although different marketing books give different figures. Michael Thomas's *Pocket Guide to Marketing* (Oxford: Basil Blackwell and *The Economist*, 1986), states that 'About 80 per cent of all new products never become commercial successes' (p. 86). The figure is presumably even higher for new product *concepts*, but these are often abandoned during the market research or test marketing phases, and never achieve a full commercial launch.)

TAPESCRIPT

Interviewer You're responsible for operational management, the management of people, but not product development. Could you say something about the role of head office?

Steve Moody Obviously, head office, the nature of what head office does in terms of selecting the products and then deciding on the quantities they buy. Obviously when they do that we have great success stories, that we develop a new product, say it's a new food recipe dishes that we introduce, it might be a new tie range, or foods from the Far East, and we introduce that and it sells very well and obviously that's fine, and usually head office don't require a lot of feedback on that. However, they could buy a particular new type of fabric, say it's a lycra fabric which we've not used before and we develop a range of ladies' underwear, for example, with that, we buy large quantities of it, we display it, we think it's the right price, we think we've chosen the right colour, everybody in head office actually thinks it's going to sell really well. It then goes out to 50 stores and for some unknown reason the customers don't want to buy it. So in those cases obviously we have a commitment there of stock that we've bought, we need to do some investigation as to find out why it's not selling and therefore head office would then come and talk to us and not simply to me but my sales staff to say, well, you know, what have we got wrong here, is it the make-up of the fabric, is it the colour of the fabric, is it the texture, is it the price, and obviously try and take some remedial action, in terms of is it price, then maybe we would reduce the price. If it's colour we would go and see

ANSWERS

1 It decides which products M&S stores are going to sell, and determines the quantity of these products that the chain will buy.
2 Ladies' (women's) underwear in a new type of fabric (lycra).
3 In these circumstances, it would have been head office that had not done sufficient market research before deciding to introduce this product, concerning the fabric, its colour, its texture, and its price.
4 The sales staff (who regularly talk to customers).
5 They could perhaps reduce the price, or change the colours offered.
6 The individual stores communicate with head office every day, and feed back a lot of information.

Vocabulary note *Fabric*, in English, means a textile from which clothes, curtains, etc. are made. There is a similar sounding word in many European languages (*Fabrik, fabrique*, etc.) that translates the English word *factory*.

2b Case study: Market research

There are no definitive answers, but here are some suggestions.

1 A department store chain would presumably have been selling other lines of swimwear, and so will have a lot of data available for analysis. There may also be sales data available in the clothing industry trade press, and perhaps statistical publications produced by the textile industry. Yet as Steve Moody's example from Marks & Spencer suggests, it might be advisable to talk to experienced sales staff, and to some target customers in focus group interviews.

2 The company launching Fresh Fries has presumably studied figures for sales of fries in different countries, perhaps those published by fast-food companies, or by potato traders. Figures must also be available from vending machine operators. It would, of course, also be necessary to test the product produced by the prototype machine with as many potential customers as possible before manufacturing the machines.

3 A company launching a new range of up-market hi-fi equipment would probably already have sales data concerning earlier ranges. It would look for data from other manufacturers, and perhaps from official industry publications. If other manufacturers did not reveal many figures, more would be available from retailers. The opinions of experienced salespeople would obviously be useful.

4 Publishers of successful dictionaries often include sales figures in their advertising ('Over three million copies sold a year'), which probably encourages competitors to enter the market. Since writing a dictionary takes a long time and a lot of people, and so requires a large financial investment, a potential publisher would gather a lot of data from a number of countries, perhaps from publishers, certainly from major distributors and retailers. They would probably also seek the opinions of applied linguists and English language teachers of the dictionaries already on the market.

New words in this unit

data	marketing mix
discount	packaging
distribution	personal selling
distribution channel	point of sale
features	producer market
focus group	promotion
head office	publicity
intuition	questionnaire
market opportunity	sales promotion
market research or	sales staff
marketing research	secondary data
market segmentation	selling
marketer	target customer

Unit 11 | Advertising

All language learners, as consumers or potential consumers, have some experience of advertising, and will probably have more to say on this subject than, say, financial derivatives or monetary policy. This unit contains an exercise concerning the different advertising media; a text about how organizations advertise their products or services; a discussion about the necessity and ethics of advertising; a listening exercise based on authentic radio commercials; and an exercise involving the preparation of a radio commercial. Vocabulary task **1a**, which illustrates the different advertising media, leads naturally into the subject.

1 Ways of advertising

1a Vocabulary

> **ANSWERS**
>
> **a** a poster on a hoarding (GB) or billboard (US)
> **b** a newspaper ad
> **c** a TV commercial
> **d** a cinema advertisement
> **e** sponsorship
> **f** a radio commercial
> **g** a classified advertisement in a newspaper (small ads in a special section of the paper)
> **h** a sandwich-board man

The price of sponsoring a good Formula 1 racing team is enormous. Ferrari's 2001 budget was estimated to be $350 million and Maclaren's $250 million. But the sponsors get many hours of television coverage, and many pictures and mentions in newspapers and magazines. Of the advertising media illustrated, national television is probably the most expensive, followed by pages in national newspapers,

and a nationwide campaign involving posters on advertising hoardings. Radio advertising – certainly *local* radio advertising – and cinema advertising are usually cheaper, as they reach a smaller audience. Classified ads in local newspapers do not cost very much, and sandwich-board men are generally not highly paid.

You may wish to discuss advertising at this point, before reading the text. Since we are all exposed to advertising, all learners will (or should) have something to say about it.

Some possible discussion questions

1 How many ads do you think you see or hear on an average day?
    (*Answer:* It is often claimed that people in towns are potentially exposed to 2,000 advertising messages a day.)

2 How many times do you think you have to see an ad or a brand name before you remember it?

3 How many times do you have to see an ad before it begins to annoy you?

4 What makes an advertisement memorable?
    humour? originality? the use of famous actors or personalities? endless repetition? nudity? other elements?

5 Do you find the advertisements on television generally:
    informative? persuasive? amusing?
    well-made? artistic? worth watching?
    an annoying interruption to the programmes?
    sometimes better than the programmes?

6 Give examples of ads that you have enjoyed.

7 Give examples of ads that have persuaded you to buy the product.

8 Do these examples coincide?

9 Are you able to *ignore* commercials on television? at the cinema?   ads in newspapers and magazines? on poster hoardings?

1b Reading

ANSWERS

1 The best kind of advertising is probably what is known as word-of-mouth advertising, when people tell their friends about a good new product or service.

2 Because they are specialists, with large resources, and staff with expert knowledge.

3 The company agrees a budget with the agency, and gives it a brief, i.e. a statement of the overall objectives of the advertising campaign, and the message it wants to communicate. The agency creates the ads and develops a media strategy.

4 The choice of which media to use for an advertising campaign, with what frequency, and in what proportions.

5 Because after a while the message will have been conveyed to virtually all potential customers, and because after a certain point people no longer notice ads, or become annoyed by their endless repetition.

1c Vocabulary

ANSWERS

1 word-of-mouth advertising   2 institutional or prestige advertising   3 advertising agencies
4 an account   5 an advertising budget
6 a brief   7 advertising campaign
8 target customers or target market
9 media planners   10 the threshold effect
11 the comparative-parity method
12 counter-cyclical advertising

Vocabulary note In Britain, *media* is plural, so, for example, television is a *medium*. In the US, *media* is sometimes also used as a singular.

1d Discussion

See page 177 of the Student's Book for the true figures from the *Harvard Business Review* survey.

The Gary Larson **cartoon** perhaps relates to statement 7, or merely to the fact that there seem to be *so many* television ads for washing powder that 'washes whiter' in almost every country in the world.

2 Radio commercials

2a Listening

ANSWER

The first ad is for Business Class air travel between England and the USA; the second is for *What Hi-Fi?* magazine; and the third is for a 'festival' in a chain of Italian restaurants.

2b Commercial 1

TAPESCRIPT

On Continental Airlines Business First, the champagne will cool you, the First Class electronic sleeper seat with extra leg room and personal video will calm you, the limousine will collect you and take you to the airport, and another will meet you in the USA, all for a Business Class fare. Business First. London, Gatwick and Manchester to New York, or London to Houston, and on to over a hundred US cities. Be cool, calm and collected.

English for Business Studies Second Edition
© Cambridge University Press 2002

ANSWERS

1 The champagne, the sleeper seat with plenty of leg room, and the limousines which take you to and from the airport.
2 The champage will cool you, the seat will calm you.
3 The three words (in the form of adjectives) make up a common English expression: 'to be cool, calm and collected', meaning to be wholly relaxed and unstressed.
4 Be cool, calm and collected.
5 Background music.

2c Commercial 2 🔊

TAPESCRIPT

Voiceover A typical horror story.

Customer Hello, I'd like to buy a stereo, please.

Salesman Certainly, madam. May I recommend the Shannon X-13 with quadruple bass boost, magnum force…

(*Woman screams*)

Voiceover If only she'd read *What Hi-Fi?*, the magazine that takes all the worry and guesswork out of buying home entertainment systems, from all-in-ones to home cinema and hi-fi separates, *What Hi-Fi?*'s test results cover all aspects of the market. What hi-fi magazine should you read? *What Hi-Fi?*

English for Business Studies Second Edition
© Cambridge University Press 2002

ANSWERS

1 The horror is the hi-fi salesman who uses a huge amount of technical jargon that the customer cannot understand at all.

2 Because, the ad is saying, no one can understand the typical hi-fi salesman, so instead you should read the magazine, which tests and recommends hi-fis, and similar products.
3 The ad mentions *all-in-ones* (more commonly known as *stereos*), i.e. hi-fi systems, usually including a CD or record player, a cassette tape recorder, a radio or tuner, and loudspeakers; *hi-fi separates*, which could include all the above sold as separate components, and *home cinema*, which would be some kind of wide-screen television and video recorder.

Note Some learners may object to the sexual stereotyping here: men obsessed with technical data and jargon, women incapable of understanding technical data and jargon.

2d Commercial 3 🔊

TAPESCRIPT

Mamma Amalfi Café-Bar Ristorante is running a festival of good Italian living, concentrating on the foods and wines of Italy, from the 25th of September to the 15th of October. Mamma Amalfi, situated at Hatfield Gallerias, Lakeside Shopping Centre, Edgware, Croydon, The Grafton Centre in Cambridge, and now open in Ealing. Mamma Amalfi, the home of good Southern Italian home cooking. At value for money prices.

English for Business Studies Second Edition
© Cambridge University Press 2002

ANSWER

1 By the use of Italian mandolin music. Another possibility would have been to give the speaker a noticeable Italian accent.

Note With an advanced class, one could do some 'literary' analysis of the language of the third ad here. 'Mamma Amalfi' is a rather smaller organization than Continental Airlines, and its ad is full of 'ad-speak'. What other aspects of 'good Italian living' apart from

'foods and wines' could its 'festival' include? What does it offer the rest of the year if it is not 'the foods and wines of Italy'? Do people really go to restaurant chains for 'good home cooking'?
Another question – why doesn't an ad for 'Mamma Amalfi's' use a woman's voice?

2e Scripting a radio commercial

It would, of course, be preferable to give learners the time to find any music or sound effects that they need, and to record their radio commercials. The class, or even other classes, could then be invited to judge which is the best commercial (and, of course, to justify their choice).

> See also the role play 'Sponsorship' in *Business Roles* by John Crowther-Alwyn, and the simulation 'Advertising Albion' in *Decisionmaker* by David Evans (Cambridge University Press).

New words in this unit

advertisement or advert or ad	institutional or prestige advertising
advertising account	media plan
advertising agency	media space
advertising campaign	message
brief	opportunities to see
budget	prospective customer
commercial	reach
comparative-parity method	sales revenue
cost per thousand	sponsorship
counter-cyclical advertising	target market
diminishing returns	threshold effect
frequency	turnover
	word-of-mouth advertising

Unit 12 | Promotional tools

As mentioned at the beginning of the unit in the Student's Book, companies have to develop good products or services, price them attractively, and make them accessible to their target customers. But this is not enough: they also have to use various promotional tools to generate sales. According to a classification used in most marketing textbooks, advertising is only one of four standard promotional tools, the others being sales promotions, public relations, and personal selling. This unit begins with a second extract from the interview with Jogishwar Singh, concerning the promotions strategies used in the launch of Fresh Fries, the product discussed in Unit 9. This is followed by a text on promotional tools, and a short case study asking the learners how they would promote various new products or services.

1 Promoting a new product

The listening section is based on a further extract from the interview with Jogishwar Singh that featured in Unit 9. If there has been a long gap between the learners doing Unit 9 and this unit, it might be a good idea to ask them to recall what they know about Fresh Fries (or to remind them!) before beginning the listening activity.

1a Listening 🔊

> **TAPESCRIPT**
>
> *Interviewer* How do you expect potential customers to become aware of Fresh Fries? Are they just going to walk down the street and see these machines?
>
> *Jogishwar Singh* That is correct. You know the machines will be painted, as you can see from the picture, in very bright fast-food colours,

which is red and yellow. I'm sure you have to really make an effort in order to miss such a machine if it is placed on the path around which you will be, and you know we will place many of them, even the test machines, we will put them in and around Piccadilly Circus, so I'm sure people will notice them.

Interviewer So the location is important?

Jogishwar Singh It is important, yes.

Interviewer Advertising and publicity would be really secondary, or…

Jogishwar Singh Well, I wouldn't say it's secondary, but I think it is more important, you know, that once…we are not really launching a media blitz until our test machines are out, and we have digested the lessons from the first series of 25 machines. Then, we've been talking to some television chains, you know, who are very much interested in the product, and they are, they have already confirmed to us that they are willing to make short programmes that they will broadcast on their business news. Now that is all free publicity for us, you know. We are counting on the novelty of the product to get us free time on television, and so that we can concentrate… We will also have paid advertising, but you know, according to our experts, the best advertising we can get is to get people to taste the fries, so we prefer to give these machines free for three months for trial, so you know, the operator gets them free for three months, and I think that is a much better advertising strategy.

Interviewer Absolutely. Your publicity strategy got me here. I saw you on the front page of a newspaper…

Jogishwar Singh Which incidentally, I didn't tell the newspaper to put our picture, he seemed to like my turban…

English for Business Studies Second Edition
© Cambridge University Press 2002

1b Comprehension

Vocabulary note A great many French, Italian and Spanish speakers habitually use the word *publicity* when they mean *advertising*, because their languages use *publicité*, *pubblicizzare* and *publicidad* for both advertising and publicity. (An alternative French translation of *publicity* is *relations publiques*, which does not help French learners to grasp the concept of paid advertising and unpaid – or indirectly paid-for – publicity.)

2 Promotional strategies

The beginning of the reading text refers back to a notion (the marketing concept) introduced in Unit 10. A class which has already studied promotion in a marketing course in their own language would probably be able to provide much of the information included in this text themselves. You could elicit this information and provoke discussion by asking questions such as:

● Do you know what we mean by the 'four Ps' of marketing?
● In what different ways can companies promote their products and services?
● What are sales promotions?
● What are the standard stages of the product life cycle?

If the learners know about promotions (and they should do – they are also consumers), the discussion question in **2c** could also be done in class before the text is read, and the reading exercise be given as homework.

2a Reading

Notes
1 & 7 We aim at a target, but cannot say 'aimed customers'.
3 Learners familiar with the plural *media* but not the singular *medium* might put *channel* here, but this is not normal English usage.
5 The noun *trial* (from the verb *to try*) appears in exercise **1a**. The other meaning of trial (in a law court) is perhaps more common.
8 Brand loyalty is obviously ulterior to brand awareness. An intermediate stage (for consumers rather than distributors) is often described as brand preference.

2b Summarizing

Learners can be asked to complete these sentences either verbally (working in pairs), or in writing (alone or working in pairs). Typical answers might be something like the following:

1 When a new product is launched, the producer has to inform customers about its existence and develop brand awareness.
2 Promotion is one of the four elements of the marketing mix; sales promotions are one of four different promotional tools.
3 The advantages of publicity include the fact that it is much cheaper than advertising, and can have a better impact, because it seems that people are more likely to read and believe publicity than advertising.

4 The four stages of the standard product life cycle (excluding the pre-launch development stage) are introduction, growth, maturity and decline.

5 Reasons to offer temporary price reductions include attracting price-conscious brand-switchers, offsetting a promotion by a competitor, and, for stores, attracting customers by way of 'loss leaders'.

6 Sales promotions need not only be aimed at customers; they can also be used with distributors, dealers and retailers, and with a company's sales force.

7 Apart from selling a company's products, sales representatives bring information back to a company from its customers, including ideas for new products.

2c Discussion

Different consumers are susceptible to different sales promotions. Some people, for example, will happily buy reduced price articles, but can't be bothered or are too embarrassed to cut out and present low-value coupons to get a reduction at the till. Some people regularly take part in promotional contests and competitions – and regularly win. Other people are too lazy to enter competitions, or too embarrassed to enter a shop and fill in a competition form without buying anything. Some people stock up on products that they use regularly when they see price reductions. Other consumers do not have the imagination, or the money, or the storage space to take advantage of such offers. And so on.

2d Vocabulary

> ### ANSWERS
>
> This exercise contains vocabulary from Units 9–12. These answers are not definitive; learners may think of other logical ways of linking the words.
>
> 1 *Advertising, publicity* and *sales promotion* are all promotional tools; <u>competitors</u> are not.

2 An *advertising agency* elaborates an *advertising campaign*, including a *media plan*; <u>word-of-mouth advertising</u> takes place among consumers, without the need for an advertising agency or campaign.

3 *Advertising managers, marketing managers* and *sales reps* work for companies; <u>brand-switchers</u> are consumers who are not loyal to particular brands.

4 *After-sales service, guarantees* and *optional features* are all elements of an extended conception of a product; <u>points of sale</u> are not.

5 *Brand awareness, brand preference* and *brand loyalty* are all stages in consumers' responses to a brand; there is no necessary relation with <u>brand name</u>.

6 *Competitions, coupons* and *free samples* are all sales promotions; <u>line-stretching</u> is not.

7 *Credit terms, discount* and *list price* are all related to a product's price; <u>packaging</u> is part of the product.

8 The product life cycle has *introduction, growth* (maturity) and *decline* stages. <u>Product improvement</u> may take place during the maturity stage, but is not a stage as such.

9 *Focus group interviews, internal research* and *questionnaires* are all market research tools; a <u>media plan</u> is not.

10 *Product, place* and *promotion* are three of the 'four Ps' of marketing; <u>packaging</u> is not.

2e Case study: Promotional strategies

How long the groups will need to elaborate a promotions strategy will depend on how inspired they are, but enough time must be left for them to present their product or service and promotional strategy to the rest of the class. It is important that they first define exactly what their product is, and preferably what differentiates it from competing products. They could perhaps be invited to use a mixture of advertising, publicity, and sales promotions. There are clearly no right answers, though you can offer opinions.

2f Discussion

Source: 'New Approach Proposed for Marketing Mix', *Business Day* (South Africa), 15 February 2000, via the Global Archive in the *Financial Times'* website www.ft.com.

I found this article by accident. The ideas in Keller's MBA dissertation do not seem to have been taken up by any other newspapers.

The answer to the question whether these new Ps would have been suggested if the words didn't begin with the letter P in English is almost certainly negative, but some of them are interesting. There can be no 'right answers' here, but good students might have interesting things to say concerning people, process, physical evidence, positioning and profit in relation to their taxis, health club, jeans, watches or potatoes.

Role play

Here is an additional, photocopiable role play.

Marketing your business school

Imagine that your past or present business school or faculty or department has invited present and former students to come up with ideas for marketing it.

You are probably not in a position to alter the school's price, and almost certainly not its place (unless you decide to do something like offering courses on the internet) so your job involves either promoting the existing 'product' or changing it.

If you decide on *promotion*, you should (obviously) first consider your target: who are you trying to reach – potential students, their parents, wealthy former students (for donations, as often happens in the USA), prospective employers, the government, etc.? Are you going to concentrate on paid advertising, on publicity, or what? If it's a matter of publicity, be specific: how are you going to achieve this?

There are two ways of conceiving the 'product' of a business school. Either it is the students who graduate from it – in other words, *you* – and the professors are just part of the 'machinery', or you are the consumer and the product is the courses you receive. Either way, if you want to change the product or the programme, be specific. Should the course be longer or shorter? Should it include more or less specialization in a particular field (marketing, finance, information technology, whatever)? Should courses be offered in more than one language? Should there be a traineeship in a company? Should the students have to write a research paper or a dissertation? Should there be an opportunity of spending a term or a semester in a different university or college abroad? And so on.

Make your plans in small groups, and then present them to the class.

English for Business Studies Second Edition
© Cambridge University Press 2002

Notes This role play will work best with groups of business school learners in the later years of their degree course. First-year students will probably have fewer ideas or less information on this subject.

Groups of three are probably best for this activity. Fifteen or 20 minutes is probably adequate for the groups to make their suggestions, during which time the teacher should go from group to group, encouraging them, and perhaps helping out with further suggestions, depending on what actually happens (or fails to happen) in a particular business school. The groups could either report back to the whole class one after another, before any discussion, or the whole class could be invited to discuss each group's suggestions in turn. There is, however, a risk of a free-for-all after only one group has reported back, if everyone has suggestions as to how to improve their business school, but a heated discussion would be fine – as long as it happens in English, is made up of constructive proposals, and involves a majority of the learners.

The teacher is of course directly implicated in the business school, and probably knows more about why it is the way it is than the learners. This does not mean that the learners will not have valid or plausible suggestions, although it might be necessary to insist that the aim is not at all to criticize other teachers' courses.

An additional **writing** activity, either individually or in groups, would be to write a page of proposals for promoting the product or service in case study **2e**, or for either publicizing the institution or altering the product in the role play here.

New words in this unit

brand awareness	planning
brand loyalty	positioning
coupon	price-conscious
decline stage	process
growth stage	promotional tool
introduction stage	public relations
loss leader	sales force
maturity stage	salespeople
media	sample
medium	trial

Test 2 | Production and marketing

Part One: Vocabulary

1 **Many writers on production argue that a lack of quality can be more expensive than achieving high quality. Which of the following costs could be saved by producing perfect quality goods?**

a advertising
b after-sales service
c dealing with complaints
d developing brand awareness
e identifying the causes of defects
f implementing corrective action
g inspecting
h inventory costs
i losing customers' goodwill
j pricing policy
k product improvement
l public relations expenses
m redesigning a product or system
n replacing products in accordance with a warranty or guarantee
o research and development
p sales promotions
q scrapping or repairing or servicing defective products
r testing

2 **Classify the following aspects of marketing according to which 'P' (*product, price, promotion, and place*) they belong to.**

advertising	guarantee	points of sale
after-sales service	inventory	publicity
brand name	market coverage	quality
credit terms	optional features	sales promotions
characteristics	packaging	size
discounts	payment period	style
distribution channel	personal selling	transportation

English for Business Studies Second Edition
© Cambridge University Press 2002

product	price	promotion	place
....	....	....	....
....	....	....	....
....	....	....	....
....		....	....
....			....
....			
....			
....			
....			

3 Which terms are defined below?

1 A company that handles advertising for clients.

2 A consumer's choice of a particular brand instead of competing products.

3 A group of potential customers interviewed about a new product concept.

4 'Advertising' that takes place when satisfied consumers tell their friends about a product or service.

5 An advertisement displayed on a billboard or hoarding.

6 Consumers' commitment to a particular brand.

7 Consumers' knowledge of the existence of a brand.

8 Consumers who don't regularly buy a particular brand, but change between competing products.

9 Favourable mention of a company's products in the media, not directly paid for by the company.

10 Other companies offering similar goods or services to the same potential customers.

11 Products given free to consumers (usually in a small size), to encourage them to try them.

12 The choice of which media to use in an advertising campaign, in order to reach the target audience.

English for Business Studies Second Edition
© Cambridge University Press 2002

Part Two: Speaking

Allocate each learner one of the following subjects, to speak about for *two minutes*, after ten minutes of preparation with the Student's Book and their course notes.

1 What are the advantages of keeping a large inventory?
2 What are the disadvantages of keeping a large inventory?
3 What is just-in-time production?
4 What is marketing?
5 What are the four major promotional tools?
6 What kind of sales promotions are available to retailers?
7 How do companies usually organize an advertising campaign?

Part Three: Composition

Possible composition titles:

1 What are the advantages and disadvantages for a manufacturing company of having a large inventory?
2 What is the 'marketing concept' (as opposed to the 'selling concept')? Is it realistic to imagine that marketing can make selling entirely superfluous?
3 To what extent can a multinational company centralize its marketing function?
4 What makes an effective advertisement?
5 In what ways can producers or retailers try to persuade customers to try new products?

ANSWERS

Part One: Vocabulary

1 b, c, e, f, g, i, m, n, q

2

product	price	promotion	place
after-sales service	credit terms	advertising	distribution channel
brand name	discounts	personal selling	inventory
characteristics	payment period	publicity	market coverage
guarantee		sales promotions	points of sale
optional features			transportation
packaging			
quality			
size			
style			

3 1 advertising agency   2 brand preference   3 focus group   4 word-of-mouth advertising
   5 poster   6 brand loyalty   7 brand awareness   8 brand-switchers   9 publicity
   10 competitors   11 samples   12 media plan

Unit 13 | Accounting and financial statements

Bookkeeping and accounting – the recording of transactions, the elaboration of budgets, the calculation of costs and expenses, the preparation of financial statements and tax returns, and so on – is central to all commercial activity, from the smallest sole-trader or self-proprietorship (one-person business) to the largest multinational company. Financial control is equally crucial for all non-commercial organizations and institutions. This unit begins with an exercise defining the different areas of accounting. There is an interview with an American accountant; a text on corporate accounting and financial statements; and an exercise based on authentic financial statements from Nokia.

All business students are likely to have followed courses in accounting early on in their studies, or even at secondary school, and so will probably be able to launch straight into exercise **1a**.

1 Types of accounting

1a Vocabulary

> **ANSWERS**
>
> 1 B 2 C 3 D 4 G 5 A
> 6 E 7 F

1b Listening 🔊

Learners could first read the questions, then listen to the interview, answer the questions in pairs, and then listen again before the answers are checked with the whole class.

Sarah Brandston mentions the IRS. This is the Internal Revenue Service, which collects taxes from individuals and businesses in the United States.

TAPESCRIPT

Sarah Brandston I'm Sarah Brandston. I am an Enrolled Agent, which in America is a person who has been certified by the IRS as an expert in all areas of taxation. I operate a business that employs two or more people in addition to myself, that concentrates on filing income tax returns and other forms required by the federal and local governments related to income taxes and sales taxes, for my clients.

I tell people, on the most basic level, a lot of my clients are young people who are just starting out, and often they have no idea at all what's involved, they might be talented in a certain field, they might be a good graphic designer, or might be a media person, or a writer, but that doesn't mean they know how to run a business. The first thing I try and do is ease them on and tell them that the basic rule for accounting, in terms of their business, is that they have to keep records that accurately reflect their financial life, the life, the financial life in the business, and the records have to be accurate enough so that we together can file a tax return from them. That's the bottom line, that's really all it's about. Then you go and you get into more complex forms of bookkeeping for corporations or partnerships, which have to follow both the generally accepted rules that are put out by the American Institute of Certified Public Accountants, and the rules that change on a daily basis that we get from the IRS.

Bookkeeping is keeping good accounts, period, it's just taking what comes in, it's looking at how much income comes in, and it's looking at what's going out, and then

---

further breaking down what goes out into the various categories that I've told them are important for tax purposes. So I usually say, in terms of their bookkeeping that they should set up categories that make sense to them in their business. They wouldn't want entertainment with office supplies, they wouldn't want books and periodicals with car expenses, it's just what I think are those common sense…bookkeeping is really a common sense way of keeping track of the income and expenses.

Interviewer The kind of companies you work with, can you just describe the sort of range of companies that you work with, and the kind of input you give them. I assume you see them sort of more than once a year?

Sarah Brandston Right. In terms of the people that I do, my clients who have their own businesses, be they self-proprietorships or small corporations or partnerships, most of the people I deal with are in creative fields. I have several film makers, I have architects and people who consult in the computer field, what I think of as my corporations, and music, those are the kind of people I think of. They're generally people that are not comfortable with doing bookkeeping, or accounting, nor do they have enough revenue in their companies that they want to, or that they're able to, pay the type of accountant that needs to see them on a monthly basis, and charge them a minimum of twenty four hundred dollars a year, let's say, to do all the accounting, the bookkeeping, and the tax preparation for them, so I try and keep my costs low so people can function, continue to function as a business…

English for Business Studies Second Edition
© Cambridge University Press 2002

ANSWERS

1 She mentions graphic designers, media people, writers, film makers, architects, people who consult in the computer field, and people who work in music.

2 She says that her clients are generally talented in their field, but they don't necessarily know how to run a business, how to do bookkeeping, or how to keep accounting records that will allow them to file tax returns.

3 Keeping records that reflect the financial life in the business accurately enough to enable one to file a tax return.

4 Corporations and partnerships.

5 She means that businesses should set up bookkeeping categories that allow them to record their expenses logically, according to what the expenses are and what the business does.

1c Discussion

My experience of teaching business students is that during the first two years of their studies they virtually all insist that they will *never* work in accounting, because it's *boring*, and then in their final semester about half of them go for job interviews with auditing companies!

The qualities required for bookkeeping are probably accuracy and concentration, and mathematical (or at least arithmetical) ability. Managerial and cost accounting require analytical ability and mathematical competence. Tax accounting probably requires a thorough knowledge of tax laws and accounting combined with a desire to help one's clients reduce their tax liabilities. Auditing presumably requires strong analytical and synthetic skills, and honesty; creative accounting presumably requires the same, with the substitution of dishonesty for honesty.

2 Company accounts

2a Vocabulary

These are all basic and important terms related to accounting. Unfortunately, several of them differ in British and American English. Fortunately, business students are likely to be familiar with most of these terms in their own language, and so should not have too many problems with understanding the concepts.

ANSWERS

1 shareholders or stockholders   2 earnings or income   3 liabilities   4 turnover
5 assets   6 depreciation or amortization
7 debtors or accounts receivable   8 creditors or accounts payable   9 stock or inventory
10 overheads or overhead

2b Reading

ANSWERS

1 assets   2 stock or inventory
3 depreciation or amortization
4 shareholders or stockholders   5 earnings or income   6 turnover   7 overheads or overhead   8 liabilities   9 debtors or accounts receivable   10 creditors or accounts payable

Vocabulary note The text begins with the phrase 'In accounting, it is always assumed…'. Accountants (like economists!) make a lot of assumptions. It is often necessary to mention to French speakers that the English verb *to assume* does not have the same meaning as the French verb *assumer*, which translates as to take responsibility for something.

The **cartoon** clearly relates to the practice known as 'creative accounting' or 'window dressing'. Learners who know something about accounting can be asked whether they find this cartoon only slightly exaggerated, or an insult to the accounting profession.

2c Summarizing

POSSIBLE ANSWERS

1 Companies record their fixed assets at historical cost because they do not need to know their real value: if the company is a going concern they are not for sale.

2 Historical cost accounting usually underestimates the value of assets that appreciate (gain value), such as land and buildings (US: real estate).

3 Countries with a regularly high rate of inflation generally use a system of current cost or replacement cost accounting, which records assets at the price that would have to be paid to replace them.

4 Company profits are usually split three ways: into tax (corporation tax in Britain, income tax in the US), dividends, and retained earnings.

5 Double-entry bookkeeping requires that every transaction is recorded in one account as a sum received and another as a sum paid.

6 A company's net assets consist of its assets minus liabilities.

7 A company's stock market capitalization is usually more than the value of its net assets, because this figure does not include intangible elements such as goodwill.

8 Flows of cash both in and out of the company are recorded in the source and application of funds statement.

3 Financial statements

ANSWERS

1 Costs and expenses   2 Income tax
3 Net profit   4 Intangible assets
5 Inventories   6 Retained earnings
7 Long-term liabilities   8 Accrued expenses
9 Net cash from operating activities
10 Cash and cash equivalents at beginning of period

Note A good time to look at the material on **numbers** in the Language reference section might be before or after this unit and the following unit on banking.

New words in this unit

accountancy	historical cost
accountant	accounting
accounting	income
accounting equation	intangible assets
accrued expenses	interest
annual report	liabilities
assets	managerial accounting
auditing	market capitalization
balance sheet	market value
bookkeeping	net book value
cash flow	nominal value
cost accounting	overheads (GB) or
creative accounting	overhead (US)
credit	partnership
creditors (GB) or	profit and loss account
accounts payable	(GB) or income
(US)	statement (US)
debit	reserves
debt	retained earnings
debtors (GB) or	revenue
accounts receivable	self proprietorship
(US)	share capital
depreciation (GB) or	share premium (GB)
amortization (US)	or paid-in surplus
dividend	(US)
double-entry	shareholders (GB) or
bookkeeping	stockholders (US)
earnings	source and application
expenses	of funds statement
financial statement	statement of changes
financial year	in financial
finished products	position
fixed asset	stock (GB) or
funds flow statement	inventory (US)
going concern	tax accounting
goodwill	work in progress

Unit 14 Banking

Like advertising, personal banking is something with which most language learners are likely to be familiar. This unit begins with a vocabulary exercise defining various basic terms related to personal banking, and continues with a text about the banking industry today, covering commercial banks, investment banks, financial deregulation, interest rates, and Eurocurrencies. There is also a role play, in which groups of young business people have to try to persuade a local bank to lend them money.

1 Personal banking

1a Vocabulary

> **ANSWERS**
>
> 1 overdraft   2 credit card   3 cash dispenser or ATM   4 loan   5 standing order or direct debit   6 mortgage   7 cash card   8 home banking   9 current or checking account   10 deposit or time or notice account

1b Discussion

Most people old enough to study business English have a bank account or some sort of dealings with banks. As always, this discussion activity is probably best done in pairs or small groups.

2 The banking industry

2a Reading

With classes that already have some knowledge of banking, the reading text could also be prepared by discussion questions such as:

- What is the difference between a commercial and an investment bank?
- How are interest rates determined?
- What are Eurodollars?
- Why are there so many dollars deposited in banks outside the USA?

An additional question that can be asked after reading the text is:

- *Why* did American legislation separate commercial and investment banking?
    (*Answer:* The answer is essentially that there is a risk that if the same bank is placing money for small investors and issuing securities, it might be tempted to sell these securities to its own customers, even if this is not necessarily in their best interests.)

> **SUGGESTED ANSWERS**
>
> 1 Commercial banking
> 2 Investment banking
> 3 Universal banking
> 4 Interest rates
> 5 Eurocurrencies

Vocabulary notes It might be useful to stress the following points:

- The past tense of *lend* is *lent* (not lended).
- A person who has borrowed money has a *debt*, pronounced /det/ (i.e. the /b/ is silent).
- The charge for borrowing money, expressed as a percentage of the loan, is called *interest* (never interests with an s).
- If you don't spend your money, but leave it in the bank, you are *saving*, and not, as German speakers often mistakenly say, sparing; something spare is something you don't need, and so can perhaps give away.

– Foreign exchange in English is not called *devises* (as in French, and similar words in German and Spanish), although of course the word *device* exists, with a wholly different meaning.

2b Comprehension

ANSWER

The first summary is the best and most complete. Each summary has one sentence per paragraph of the text. The first sentence of the third summary, and the second sentence of the second summary are probably better than the equivalent sentences in the first summary, but the remainder of the second and third summaries are erroneous. Second summary: the distinction between commercial and investment banks is only 'traditional' in some countries, notably Britain and the US; only the minimum interest rate or discount rate is usually fixed by the central bank; banks can do Eurocurrency business at home as well as abroad; and Eurocurrencies are not only European – the name is misleading. Third summary: the text does not say that British banks are combining with American ones; and it is not only European banks that can do Eurodollar business.

2c Vocabulary

ANSWERS

1 deposit   2 foreign currencies   3 yield
4 liquidity   5 maturity   6 underwrite
7 takeover   8 merger   9 stockbroking
10 portfolio management   11 deregulation
12 conglomerate   13 blue chip
14 solvency   15 collateral

2d Vocabulary

ANSWERS

Common collocations include: charge interest
do business   exchange currencies
issue bonds   make loans   make profits
offer advice   offer loans   pay interest
raise funds   receive deposits
underwrite security issues

3 Getting a loan

Role play

These are the roles to be photocopied and given to the groups of learners:

ROLE 1

Your bank recently launched a big advertising campaign announcing that it was the friend of small businesses, with the result that everyone with half an idea is coming to you and asking for money! Your superiors expect you to pick out good local investment opportunities. On the other hand, you have previously lent money to young people who lost it all within six months. You want facts and figures – about costs, sales projections, profit margins, repayment periods, existing competitors, the possibility of new competitors entering the market, and the long-term prospects for the market. You are slightly worried about the meetings, because you know absolutely nothing about dance music, never order take-away pizzas, and know very little about computers. For this reason, you can invite your two assistants to the meeting if you want to.

English for Business Studies Second Edition
© Cambridge University Press 2002

ROLE 2

You are fans of this kind of music; you think you know what the market wants; you think the market is big enough to make a small shop profitable; you think the existing competition is weak – inadequate selection of music, wrong ambience, etc. But remember that you will probably be talking to someone who knows nothing at all about the kind of music you are interested in. He or she wants numbers. You have to convince him or her that your business will be successful – that it will have, and keep, enough customers to make a profit. You have to pay three months' rent in advance for the small shop. You have to buy display racks and lots of CD players and headphones. Your suppliers (record companies, importers, distributors) expect to be paid within 60 days.

English for Business Studies Second Edition
© Cambridge University Press 2002

ROLE 3

Members of the group have been working in the business – answering the telephone, making pizzas and delivering them – for over two years. You know that the business is profitable. The owner wants to leave the country quickly and is keen to sell to you. You have enough money to pay the rent and the normal bills, but the equipment will cost $50,000. Not only do you have experience in the take-away pizza business, but as business students you know all about accounting, promotions, etc.

English for Business Studies Second Edition
© Cambridge University Press 2002

ROLE 4

You are what other people call 'computer nerds'. You know everything about computers. You have spent several hours a day in front of a computer screen since you were nine years old. In fact you don't do anything else. You have been advising small local businesses for two years and earning good money, but you would like to buy better hardware for yourselves. $50,000 would be perfect.

English for Business Studies Second Edition
© Cambridge University Press 2002

Notes Three is probably the right size for a group; if the class is large, more than one group can prepare one or more of the roles, although probably only one group will be chosen to enact each role. As usual, the groups and roles can be chosen either by you or the learners. It will probably be necessary for one person to dominate each group in the actual interviews: again, who this is can be the teacher's or the group's choice. Fifteen minutes is probably long enough to prepare the roles, during which time you should make sure that the learners are following the instructions. Then the group of bankers can choose in which order to speak to the potential borrowers, while the rest of the class listens. If there is time, you could briefly talk about polite ways to begin and end interviews such as this. The bankers can choose to lend to none, one, two or all three of the groups. At the end, the class can be invited to say whether they agree with the bankers' choice.

A possible **writing** activity would be for the learners (singly, or in groups) to write an anticipated list of expenses and revenues for their business, over a two-year period, or a list of reasons why the loan will be granted by the bank, and under what conditions, or why it will be refused.

See also the role plays 'Deciding where to invest' and 'Servicing a debt' in *Business Roles 2* by John Crowther-Alwyn, and the simulation 'A year in fashion' in *Decisionmaker* by David Evans (Cambridge University Press).

New words in this unit

balance	fee
bank account	financial markets
bank transfer	foreign currency
base rate or prime rate	funds
blue chip	interest rate
bonds	international trade
borrow	investment
cash dispenser or ATM	investment bank
cashcard	issue
central bank	lend
cheque (GB) or check (US)	liquidity
	loan
collateral	maturity
commercial or retail bank	merchant bank
	merger
commission	mortgage
conglomerate	overdraft
credit card	portfolio
credit standing or credit rating or creditworthiness	profit
	property
	risk
current account (GB) or checking account (US)	securities
	share
	solvency
deposit	spread or margin
deposit account (GB) or time or notice account (US)	stockbroking
	takeovers
	underwrite
direct debit or standing order	universal bank
	withdraw
discount rate	yield
Eurocurrency	

Unit 15 | Stocks and shares

This is the first of three units about corporate finance and investment. Equities or stocks (US) or shares (GB) are one of the two main ways by which companies raise money (the other being bonds, which are covered in the following unit). The unit begins with a general discussion about different investment possibilities for people with a lot of money. This is followed by a text about company law and the issuing of stocks or shares; a listening exercise based on a television financial report; and an exercise about financial idioms frequently encountered in the press. The unit ends with a short case study concerning ethical investment.

1 Issuing stocks and shares

1a Discussion

Here's a wholly fictitious story that could be used to introduce the opening discussion task:

> Do you know how Rockefeller made his first million dollars? One day, when he was young and very poor, he was walking along the street and he found a one cent piece. He bought an apple with it, polished it on his shirt, made it look nice and shiny, and sold it for two cents. Then he bought two apples, polished them, and sold them both for two cents each, and so on. After two months, he had enough money to buy a barrow for his apples. After two years, he was just about to open his first fruit store…when he inherited a million dollars from his uncle! This is still the quickest way to get rich.

Putting your money under the mattress is probably not a good idea unless you live in a country with no investment opportunities, no inflation, no burglaries, and banks that are likely to go bankrupt. Winning the lottery would probably give you the best possible return on your money, but the odds against winning are generally enormous (e.g. about 14 million to 1 for the top prize in the British lottery). About one gambler out of eight comes away from Las Vegas with a profit. Keeping your money in a bank is generally safe, although interest rates paid to depositors are generally lower than those on the bond market, for example. The price of gold sometimes rises dramatically – for example, during financial crises – but it can also fall. Furthermore, gold pays no interest, and it costs money to store it in safety. Buying a Van Gogh gives you something to look at, but also to protect against damage and thieves. Prices of impressionist paintings have risen dramatically in the past 30 years, but they could also fall. Property (GB) or real estate (US) usually appreciates in value in the long term, but the property market is subject to speculative booms and slumps, so you have to buy at the right time (although Mark Twain's advice, 'Buy land, young man, they're not making it any more' is probably still valid). Government bonds and bonds in secure companies are generally a safe investment, but a long-term fixed-interest bond can lose a lot of value if interest rates rise sharply. Shares are more risky than bonds, as their value can fluctuate wildly (e.g. minus 30% in three days in the crash of October 1987), and because dividends, unlike bond interest payments, are not guaranteed.

Note This exercise assumes that learners know what bonds and shares are. They may know, or can be told, that bonds are generally considered to be safer than shares, but this is not the place for a long discussion on the risks and returns of different types of security, as these issues are covered in this and the following units.

1b Reading

Classes that have studied financial or economic theory may wish (or at least may be able) to discuss the **cartoon**. Are financial markets efficient, or do they work according to rumours and panic, as the cartoon suggests?

The pre-reading comprehension questions could equally be used as discussion questions. Business students often have general notions about bankruptcy, limited liability companies, shares, and the motivations of shareholders. Many learners, however, will be unfamiliar with the term *limited liability*, which is not the same as *limited responsibility*, which means being mentally impaired – unable to take on normal adult responsibilities – which is not usually an advantage for company executives.

ANSWERS

1 Because a non-incorporated business (i.e. one that is not a company) has unlimited liability for debts. If it owes money, the people involved in it are not protected from bankruptcy and can lose their personal possessions. A company provides legal protection and limited liability.

2 In order to raise capital, generally to expand the business.

3 Shares give their holders part of the ownership of a company. Shareholders receive a proportion of a company's profits as a dividend, and may be able to make a capital gain by selling their shares at a higher price than they paid for them.

Vocabulary notes

– The regular verb to *found* a company (found – founded – founded) should not be confused with the irregular verb to *find* (find – found – found).

– A bankrupt company is *wound up* (which rhymes with *sound*). This is the irregular past participle of the verb *wind (up)*, which should not be confused with the verb and noun *wound* (to injure someone), which have the same vowel sound as *soon*. (Similarly, the verb *wind*, which rhymes with *mind*, should not be confused with the noun *wind*, used when talking about the weather.)

– There is an important difference between *liability*, meaning responsibility for debts, and *liabilities*, the sum which in accounting equals a company's assets.

– All companies require registered *premises* (whether they are an office, a factory, a warehouse, a workshop, a shop, or whatever), always used as a plural.

– French speakers often confuse the nouns *vote* and *voice*, which are the same in their language.

– An *obligation* (i.e. to issue an annual report) in English is, of course, something that a person or organization *has to do*, and should not be confused with the meaning of the French word *obligation* that translates into English as *bond*.

Additional questions

1 The first line of the text mentions partnerships. What kind of people generally work in partnerships, and why?
   (*Answer:* In many countries, including Britain and the US, professional people such as lawyers, doctors and architects are not allowed to form limited companies, a law designed to make them act responsibly, because of their unlimited liability, and to make them concentrate on serving their clients rather than shareholders.)

2 The text mentions the way in which merchant banks or investment banks underwrite security issues. There are other financial organizations whose work involves underwriting different kinds of risks. What are they?
   (*Answer:* Insurance companies, which underwrite risks such as fire, accident, theft, loss, damage, injury or death.)

1c Comprehension

This short writing and comprehension exercise can easily be done, or at least checked, in pairs.

POSSIBLE QUESTIONS

1 What are the obligations of companies whose shares are traded on stock exchanges? (or '…of publicly-quoted companies')

2 What is an over-the-counter market?

3 What does a company normally do if it wishes to raise further share capital?

4 What is a bonus issue?

5 What rights do shareholders have?

1d Vocabulary

2 Stock markets

2a Listening 🔊

TAPESCRIPT

Reporter The Footsie 100 Index in London is up
23.2 points; the DAX in Frankfurt up 7.02,
but the CAC-40 in Paris is down 3.4. In New
York, stocks were firmer last night, with the
Dow-Jones climbing 37 points – that's 0.92%
– and the Nasdaq recovering 86 points.

Over on foreign exchanges the dollar has
gained a little bit over two cents against the
euro, but against the yen it's down almost
nine-tenths at 98.81. Looking at the euro, it's
up by nearly a cent against the Swiss franc,
although against the yen it remains virtually
unchanged.

A look now at trading in the bond
markets, which have staged a modest
recovery after the falls of the last few days.
The key US long bond is up six ticks: the
yield is 5.29%, while the German benchmark
long *Bund* has edged up nine thirty-seconds
to trade at 99 and five-sixteenths. It's now
yielding 4.78%.

In London this morning, gold is down
50 cents at $260.75 an ounce. In Rotterdam,
the spot price for oil is still 19.66 a barrel.

English for Business Studies Second Edition
© Cambridge University Press 2002

Note A 'tick' in bond prices means $\frac{1}{16}$ of a per cent.

An additional exercise Especially if the numbers
dictation in the Language reference section has
already been done, you could ask learners to write
down all the figures they hear. Many learners are
unfamiliar with fractions such as $\frac{5}{16}$ and $\frac{9}{32}$, and also
need practice with decimals.

2b Vocabulary

The idioms selected here are only a fraction of those
regularly used by financial journalists. Interested
learners should be encouraged to read the market
reports in a newspaper such as the *Financial Times*,
Wall Street Journal, or *International Herald Tribune*,
and, where available, to watch the financial
programmes on CNN, CNBC, etc., or listen to the
market reports on radio stations such as the BBC
World Service.

2c Vocabulary

2d Vocabulary

This exercise includes words introduced for the first time in the previous exercise, and so cannot be done before **2c**.

2e Discussion

This question comes from Fons Trompenaars' book *Riding the Waves of Culture*, already quoted in Unit 5. If the friend sold her shares on this information, she would, of course, be guilty of insider trading.

2f Case study: Ethical investments

There are clearly no definitive 'right answers' here. Some learners will insist that 'business is business' and that all these activities are acceptable. They might, however, agree that their relative, as specified in the instructions, would have a different view. (Unit 21 is on business ethics.)

New words in this unit

Annual General
    Meeting (GB) or
    Annual Meeting of
    Stockholders (US)
authorized share
    capital
bankrupt
bonus issue or scrip
    issue or
    capitalization issue
    or stock dividend
    or stock split
capital
commodity
corporation
creditor
defensive stock
equity
float
flotation
growth stock
insider share-dealing
institutional investor
legal entity
limited company
liquidate
market price
market-maker

Memorandum of
    Association (GB) or
    Certificate of
    Incorporation (US)
mutual fund
nominal value or face
    value or par value
over-the-counter
    market
owner
premises
private limited
    company
public limited
    company (GB) or
    listed company
    (US)
quoted or listed
    company
real estate
registrar of companies
rights issue
stock exchange
unlimited liability
venture capital
wind up (the Student's
    Book only has the
    past participle
    wound up)

Unit 16 | Bonds

This unit covers debt finance, or more specifically, bonds. It begins with a short and (it is hoped) humorous extract from a well-known novel. This is followed by a more difficult interview with a vice-president of a New York investment bank, who explains in more detail what bonds are, why people issue and buy them, and what causes their price to fluctuate. There is then a reading text on bonds, and a further listening which defines three different types of bonds.

1 Defining bonds

1a Reading

For a change, this reading passage, in which a hapless father tries to explain to his six-year-old daughter what bonds are, has no exercise attached. (These lines of dialogue are extracted from the novel without the intervening narrative descriptions, and so on.)

After a definition of bonds for adults in **1b**, discussion activity **1d** returns to explaining business concepts to children.

1b Listening 🔊

> **TAPESCRIPT**
>
> *Richard Mahoney* Generally speaking, bonds are obligations that are issued by companies and governments that are in essence promises to pay individuals or other investors – providers of funds – and they generally provide for a fixed rate of interest, that is a fixed repayment schedule, and a date in the future at which the money will be returned. They're different, for example, from stocks, which have an uncertain future pay-off, depending on a company's performance, and no final maturity date, so long as the company remains active and solvent.

> *Interviewer* What's J. P. Morgan's role in the bond market? Are you organizing the sale of bonds on behalf of companies, or are you also buying bonds on behalf of investors?
>
> *Richard Mahoney* J. P. Morgan has many roles in the bond market. We work with companies and governments to help them issue bonds, that is borrow money for their purposes. We also have many investor clients who are purchasing bonds for their own investment portfolios, and those investor clients would be individuals, they would also be pension funds who make investments on behalf of their members for their retirement monies. They would also be mutual funds which, in the United States, have become a very popular form of investment for individuals and constitute a very large source of savings in the country.
>
> *Interviewer* For investors, what are the advantages of bonds as opposed to other ways of investing money?
>
> *Richard Mahoney* For investors, bonds represent an investment that, generally speaking, carries a moderate degree of risk. And investors like to hold a diversified portfolio of investments, some with very very low risks, for example, government securities, where the risk of non-payment or default is very very low, whereas other parts of their portfolios would be considered much higher risk, namely investments in stocks, so bonds provide, generally speaking, a more moderately…an asset that has a moderate level of risk, although there are some bonds that are more, more safe than others, and that depends on the quality of the issuer.
>
> Investors can obtain a return on their bond investments by holding them to

maturity. These investors are usually characterized as long-term investors or buy-and-hold investors, and they would receive their return over time by receiving periodic interest payments, usually twice a year, in most structures, and then upon the maturity of the bond, getting their principal back.

The advantages of trading bonds, for an investor, and how an investor would realize their gains is through the price appreciation that may accrue to a bond during the time at which…the time during which the investor would hold it. For example, the price of a bond is directly related to the level of interest rates in the economy. If I could use a simple example, if you purchased a bond today, that bond, let's say, would have a price of one hundred. Bonds are denominated based on values of one hundred. If interest rates were to increase, that means that the investor community demands a higher price for lending their money. As a result the amount that you could invest a dollar today would yield a higher return than the value yesterday. Meaning that the bond you bought yesterday is worth slightly less, so perhaps it's worth ninety-nine. If you were to sell that bond you would then have lost one point. On the other hand, however, if interest rates fall, the value of that bond that you purchased yesterday increases. So that an investor over time may realize that invest…that bonds that were purchased today have a higher value, as a result of how interest rates have moved. They could be sold, that capital gain is similar to the gain that you would see from a share investment or a real estate investment or other things, and would be added to whatever interest you had earned over the life of holding that bond.

English for Business Studies Second Edition
© Cambridge University Press 2002

1c Vocabulary

The learners should look at this exercise before listening to the interview a second time.

1d Discussion

1 Business and economics students should have some idea of what the economy is expected to do in the foreseeable future, and whether interest rates are likely to rise or fall. Of course, no one has certain knowledge about the future path of interest rates, otherwise they could become very rich indeed…

2 The following would perhaps be vaguely comprehensible to six-year-olds:
- A bond is when you lend somebody money, like if you say, 'I'll lend you the 95¢ pocket money I've got in my piggy bank if you give me back $1 next week.' If you write that down on a piece of paper, it's a bond. Though usually it's for much, much more money. A bond dealer is someone who arranges things like this.
- Companies make things and sell them. As well as buying the things that companies make, people can also buy a part of the companies that

make them, and then they get some of the money that people give to the company when they buy things. A stockbroker is someone who buys and sells parts of companies.

- Every time a company buys or sells something, it has to write the details down in a list in a book or on a computer. An internal auditor is someone who checks all these lists to make sure that they are right.

- Companies often have a lot of people working for them. Big companies can have hundreds of people. The personnel manager is the person who looks after all these people.

- Sometimes the people who work in companies join together in what we call trade unions, which try to look after the people who join them, and try to make sure that they work in good conditions, and get a lot of money. This is the job of a trade union organizer.

- Before a company makes something and tries to sell it, it tries to find out whether people would like to buy the thing they want to make. A market researcher is someone who asks people questions about products, for example, 'Would you buy a football in the shape of a banana?' or 'Would you like a doll whose arms and legs you could take off?'

I'm sure you or your students can do better!

2 The uses of bonds

2a Reading

ANSWERS

1 The advantage of borrowing money by issuing bonds is that interest payments, unlike dividends, are tax-deductible. But interest has to be paid even in a year in which a company makes no profit, so it is safer to have equity capital as well, on which no dividends need be paid if there are no profits.

2 Governments issue bonds when their expenditures are greater than tax revenues.

2b Comprehension

ANSWERS

1 C (See first paragraph of text.)

2 C (If interest rates have gone up, bondholders may get less than they paid for a bond, and if a company seems to be going bankrupt, no one will buy their bonds at any price, hence 'try to get their money back'.)

3 B (See third paragraph, and also the last paragraph of the tapescript of the interview in 1b.)

4 C (See fourth paragraph; A is false because the advantage of bonds over bank loans is not a fiscal advantage, but a matter of borrowing costs.)

5 B (See final paragraph.)

2c Vocabulary

ANSWERS

1 F	2 E	3 A	4 B	5 G
6 C	7 D			

2d Listening and discussion: Types of bond 🔊

For a change, the answers to this exercise are *not* to be found explicitly in the interview, but require the learners to think logically, and perhaps to draw on their overall knowledge of finance.

It will probably be necessary to play each description twice, before asking the learners to answer the question (or questions) relating to a particular type of bond.

Richard Mahoney **Floating rate notes** have…
became quite popular as interest rates around the world were deregulated. There was a time in the banking system when interest rates were regulated at fixed levels and most people chose to borrow at a fixed rate of interest. Today we have many options that a borrower can choose for the way in which they will raise money. One of them is through a floating rate note, and like its name suggests, the interest rate on that bond is variable. It is usually indexed to a particular reference rate, such as the prime rate, which varies from time to time, or something called LIBOR, which is the London Inter-Bank Offered Rate, so that a holder of those notes would see the interest that they received vary over time, depending on the levels of interest rates in the market place.

A **convertible bond** is a type of bond that has features of both a traditional bond, as well as a stock. Convertible means that the bond is exchangeable for equity or stock, provided certain conditions are met. When a convertible bond is initially issued it looks like an ordinary bond, it pays a fixed interest rate, it has a final maturity date, but it also has a feature that permits the holder to redeem it for shares in the borrower, should certain conditions prevail, and normally those conditions are related to the price of the company's equity, the general level of interest rates.

Junk bonds are simply another name, the popular name if you will, for high yield securities. They are the bonds that are issued by companies that are seen to have a very high risk of default. You can think of the securities issued by the US Treasury, the US government, as being at the other end of the risk spectrum, seen as virtually immune from the risk of default. Junk bonds are at the other end of the risk spectrum, where there is seen a considerable chance of default, but as a result, investors are paid a premium to hold those securities because of their risk.

English for Business Studies Second Edition
© Cambridge University Press 2002

Notes Possible post-listening questions for the first extract on **floating rate notes**:

1 What is another word for 'floating'?
   (*Answer:* Variable.)

2 Are mortgages usually fixed or floating?
   (*Answer:* Floating; it is highly dangerous to issue a 30-year mortgage at a fixed rate of interest, as the American Savings and Loans discovered with the rise of interest rates in the mid 1970s.)

3 What does 'float' mean in relation to shares as opposed to bonds?
   (*Answer:* To float a company is to issue shares to the public for the first time, as mentioned in the previous unit.)

Junk bonds will be mentioned again in Unit 19, in relation to Michael Milken and leveraged buyouts.

ANSWERS

1 Companies would obviously be interested in issuing floating rate notes if they were confident that interest rates would fall.

2 Investors would, equally obviously, be interested in buying floating rate notes if they expected interest rates to rise.

3 Investors will be interested in convertible bonds if they expect a company's share price to rise sufficiently for them to make a profit by converting the bond into shares.

4 Since convertible bonds offer the investor the possibility of extra returns, companies are usually able to issue them at a lower than normal rate of interest. It is usually cheaper to issue bonds than shares, and convertibles give a company the advantages of debt financing (the tax shield) without the necessity to repay the principal if the bondholders later convert the bonds into shares.

5 Speculative investors who like high yields, and who calculate that the extra interest paid by junk bonds more than compensates for the possible risk of default.

See also the simulation 'Wall Street blues' in *Decisionmaker* by David Evans (Cambridge University Press).

New words in this unit

above par	income tax
appreciate	investment grade
bearer certificate	junk bond
below par	liquid
buy-and-hold	money supply
investors	pension fund
capital gains	primary market
convertible bond	principal
coupon	public spending
deal	repayment
debt financing	secondary market
debt-equity ratio	tax deductible
default	tax shield
depreciate	Treasury Bill
equity financing	Treasury Bond
floating rate note	VAT or value-added
gilt-edged securities or	tax
gilts	

Unit 17 | Futures and derivatives

Stocks and bonds have existed, in various forms, for hundreds of years. This unit covers more recent financial instruments, including futures and forward contracts, options, and swaps, these last two often being classified under the more general term of financial derivatives. Some of these instruments are rather more difficult to understand than stocks and bonds, which is why they have recently begun to appear regularly in the news, as various banks, companies, and local governments have suffered serious problems, or even bankruptcy, as a result of using derivatives.

The unit begins with an elementary vocabulary exercise, and continues with a reading text, and listening exercises based on an extract from a talk by an expert on derivatives. The unit ends with an extract from a well-known and surprisingly humorous book about the investment banking industry.

1 Defining futures and derivatives

A lead-in to the topic would be to ask learners to look at the photo of a coffee picker and then to think about why the price of coffee and similar commodities often goes up and down.

After which you could tell them the following (bad) joke:

> One morning on the trading floor of a large futures market somebody shouts 'Frost', and immediately the prices of coffee and orange juice futures rise 5%. Twenty seconds later the same voice shouts 'Frost' a second time, even louder, and coffee and orange juice prices rise another 5%. Twenty seconds later the voice shouts 'There's a telephone call for Mr Frost', and the prices immediately drop back again.

1a Vocabulary

This exercise is designed to introduce the basic key concepts before the reading. The concept of *derivatives* is perhaps the most difficult to understand. It includes options, and other investments discussed in the reading text in **1b**, including exchange rate swaps and interest rate swaps.

ANSWERS
1 B   2 A   3 F   4 C   5 E   6 D

1b Reading

After establishing the basic vocabulary (futures, options, derivatives, hedging, speculation), it may be possible to elicit some of the content of the text in **1b**, depending on the learners' knowledge.

Possible questions

1 What are the most important commodities traded on futures markets?
   (*Answer:* Gold, silver, platinum, copper, wheat, corn, oats, soya beans, potatoes, beef, pork, tea, coffee, cocoa, sugar, orange juice.)
2 Why have futures markets developed?
   (*Answer:* Because both producers of commodities, and buyers – for example, manufacturers of coffee or copper pipes – are interested in hedging to guarantee a future price; and because there are lots of speculators.)
3 Where are the major futures markets?
   (*Answer:* Chicago, London, New York, Paris, Frankfurt, Sao Paulo, etc.)

1c Summarizing

1d Vocabulary

2 The dangers of derivatives

2a Listening 🔊

It will probably be necessary, as usual, to play the first part of the listening twice before the learners answer the questions.

TAPESCRIPT

Lillian Chew If you can't measure it, you can't manage it; if you can't manage it, you can't control it; if you can't control it, you don't do it; and that's the key message coming out from some of these very high profile losses of the last two years. I'm sure that banks are as much to blame, but I think so are the end-users, in taking on risks that they just didn't understand, or misusing these derivatives for some of their own aims.

There's nothing wrong in taking on these risks if you understand them, but I think derivatives have been misused, and they have features that allow themselves to be misused.

I think both the P&G and Gibson cases show clearly that management did not have a clear policy on derivative usage, or maybe I should clarify that statement. We all know that derivative usage falls into two main categories – hedging, or to earn investment returns. A firm can use derivatives for both purposes, but the important thing is that the same transaction should not have twin objectives. You should not be hedging and trying to lower the cost of funding and then selling options to take on extra risk.

English for Business Studies Second Edition
© Cambridge University Press 2002

ANSWERS

1 False (She says the fault lies with both banks and end-users.)

2 True

3 True

4 False (She says that this is exactly what you should not do.)

2b Vocabulary 🔊

The second part of the listening can perhaps be played only once, while the learners follow the tapescript in the book. After they have answered the questions, the second part can be played again, leading straight into the third part.

TAPESCRIPT

Lillian Chew If it's a hedge you manage it passively, you don't worry too much if rates move against you or in your favour. If it's not a hedge, if it's to take on, if a derivative is used to take on risk, to increase returns, then it requires a more hands-on management approach. You need stop-loss limits, you need to conduct scenario analysis to see how that transaction behaves under various conditions, you need to conduct sensitivity analysis to see what their most sens…, what market conditions they're most sensitive to. And then you have to judge whether the P&L impact of

---

that transaction can be withstood in the firm. Or as in P&G's case whether cost savings generated are worth the open-ended exposure. I think there's also a need for management to give the front line personnel relevant guidelines for all activities.

I think the industry realizes that it has to police itself. I think they realize that if they don't police themselves the regulators will come on, on them. I think that's why we've seen the framework for voluntary oversight from the SEC-registered companies as well as ISDA's code of conduct, as well as the Bankers' Trust-Federal Reserve sales agreement. I think all these codes of conduct embody the principle that the major risks of a transaction have to be explained to customers, and that sensitivity and scenario analysis are offered unsolicited to customers, and that these analyses should be done as objectively as possible.

English for Business Studies Second Edition
© Cambridge University Press 2002

ANSWERS

1 G	2 C	3 E	4 A	5 B	6 H
7 I	8 F	9 D			

Vocabulary note French, Italian and Spanish speakers often confuse the English words *sensible* and *sensitive*, and *sensibility* and *sensitivity*, as, for example, the French for *sensitivity* is *sensibilité*.

2c Comprehension 🔊

TAPESCRIPT

Lillian Chew I'll end with the fact that the industry's image has been tarnished is a good thing, I think. I believe that if the high profile losses prod senior management of all our companies to sit up and take a greater and more active interest in how companies

---

use derivatives, that's the best possible thing. It is negligent to leave the policy framing of, to leave policy framing of derivative usage to front line managers. Managing derivative risk needs strong corporate governance, from the top, and an understanding of derivatives on the part of senior management. Peter Baring of Barings Bank did not understand derivatives. He does not own a bank any more.

English for Business Studies Second Edition
© Cambridge University Press 2002

ANSWERS

1 Possible answer: Because this will force senior managers to become more aware of the potential risks of derivatives, and therefore act more responsibly.

2 C ('I believe that if the high profile losses prod senior management of all our companies to sit up and take a greater and more active interest in how companies use derivatives, that's the best possible thing.' The verb *prod* here means encourage or oblige.)

After the learners have listened to the third part, they can be asked how the **cartoon** relates to the listening.

(*Answer:* The somewhat improbable cartoon has a manager who doesn't even know what a billion is. This is perhaps relevant to the issue of senior management's understanding of derivatives and their potential risks, e.g. the top managers of Barings Bank who allowed a single trader to build up losses of over a billion dollars.)

2d Discussion

Financial managers, investment advisers, securities traders, and professional speculators all presumably need to be good at numbers, to have a good understanding of the financial markets on which they operate, and the education and intelligence to understand which events are likely to affect asset prices. They also require the ability to act and react extremely rapidly, when faced with both expected and unexpected events. Speculators clearly also need a taste for risk, and should be able to accept inevitable losses – preferably of their own money.

Given the uncertainty of a great many financial transactions, and the complexity and large potential risks involved in many derivative instruments, there is a considerable risk that customers (or potential customers) may misunderstand or underestimate their potential liabilities, and lay themselves open to huge risks. Some people will see ethical objections to selling such instruments, others will not, perhaps according to the Latin expression *caveat emptor* – let the buyer beware. (See Unit 21 on business ethics, section **1a**.)

2e Reading

To finish the unit, here is a humorous description of the reality of futures and options trading. The majority of customers in these markets are clearly speculators rather than prudent 'investors'. If time is short, learners could be asked to read this as homework.

POSSIBLE ANSWER

Lewis clearly does not have a very high opinion of his customers. They were all speculating rather than investing, and risked losing their money 'in a heartbeat', or at least in the time it takes for an interest rate to change. He singles out the French and English as having a long history of doing crazy things with money and looking for – and believing in – improbable plans or schemes for getting rich quickly.

2f Comprehension

SUGGESTED ANSWERS

1 Lewis means that all of his customers were speculating with money rather than constructively investing, and the 'not-so-pure' speculators were presumably taking extremely dangerous and possibly illegal risks with other people's assets.

2 *Leverage* means the potential for earning – or losing – a large amount from a very small stake or down-payment.

3 Because of the huge size of potential losses, due to the leverage effect. Casinos would obviously find it very difficult to collect losses many times greater than the amount of money gamblers had with them.

New words in this unit

call option	hedging
currency swap	interest-rate swap
derivatives	leverage
exercise price or strike price	options
financial instruments	premium
fluctuate	put option
foodstuffs	speculation
forward contract	speculator
futures	spot market
hands-on management	unsolicited

Unit 18 | Market structure and competition

1 Market structure

In most industries there are larger and smaller competitors. Marketing people usually talk in terms of market leaders, market challengers, and market followers. Economists analyse markets with a different set of concepts: perfect competition, cartels, oligopolies, monopolies, and so on. This unit considers markets from both perspectives. There is a discussion about well-known market leaders; a text about leaders, challengers and followers; and exercises about perfect competition and market concentration. Discussion task **1a**, concerning goods owned by the learners and their families, is a natural lead-in to the topic.

1a Discussion

Learners are likely to know that, e.g. Coca-Cola, Levi's, Nike, Gillette, Kodak, Kelloggs, and McDonalds, are market leaders, and that Pepsi, Reebok, and so on are market challengers.

In other industries – such as automobiles, consumer electronics, white goods (fridges and cookers), cameras, and so on – they will know that there are several major manufacturers, without knowing which has the largest market share.

They will almost certainly also be able to give examples of products manufactured by market followers that they have bought, either because they were cheaper, or because they wanted something specialized.

1b Reading

POSSIBLE ANSWERS

1 Market leaders
2 Expanding markets
3 Market challengers
4 Market followers
5 Establishing a niche / Dangers faced by market followers

1c Comprehension

ANSWERS

The *second* summary is the only accurate one.

The first sentence of the *first* summary is clearly false. The last sentence of the first paragraph of the text, 'The market leader is frequently able to lead other firms in the introduction of new products', means that other companies are obliged to follow, not that the leader helps them. The last sentence is equally inaccurate: the fifth paragraph of the text says that a product that merely imitates and has no unique selling proposition is always a risk, not only during recessions.

The *third* summary is also inaccurate. The text says that a market leader is *often* the first company to have entered or to have succeeded in a field, not that the first company *nearly always* becomes the leader. The text states that market followers can choose to attack *either* the leader *or* various followers, and *not* that leaders regularly attack both challengers (in the plural) and followers. The last sentence is wholly false as the text does not state that imitating the leader's products is a safe strategy.

1d Vocabulary

ANSWERS

1 market share   2 promotions
3 monopoly   4 competitors   5 slogan
6 market segmentation   7 niche
8 differential advantage   9 turnover
10 recession

2 Competition

The first section of this unit considered markets as they are usually seen by businesses – largely in terms of market share, and competition between specific companies, e.g. the leader, challenger and well-known followers in particular industries. The second section considers competition and market structure from the viewpoint of economists, who talk in the abstract about perfect competition, monopoly, monopolistic competition, and so on.

2a Vocabulary

ANSWERS

1 perfect competition   2 monopoly
3 monopsony   4 natural monopoly
5 monopolistic competition   6 oligopoly
7 economies of scale   8 barriers to entry
9 dominant-firm oligopoly   10 cartel

2b Comprehension

ANSWERS

1 a monopsony (the government should be the only buyer)
2 an oligopoly
3 perfect competition

4 monopolistic competition (because of consumer preference for several marginally different brands, which creates fragmented markets too small to allow many competitors)
5 a dominant-firm oligopoly (IBM – although, of course, mainframes have now widely been replaced by smaller computers)
6 a monopoly (regarding ownership of the railway tracks, if not always train services)

2c Reading

ANSWERS

First paragraph: L, J, F, M, I
Second paragraph: D, C, B
Third paragraph: K, H, G, E, A

2d Discussion

There are, of course, no 'right' answers here. Most of the ideas in the second and third paragraphs are to be found in the writings of a particular group of economists known as the 'Austrian School', who are much more sympathetic to entrepreneurs, market concentration, and even monopoly, than many other economists, and who are strongly opposed to government intervention in markets. Many other economists would judge their ideas somewhat extreme. For example, the 'soon' in sentence H is debatable, especially if the entrepreneur has a monopoly, either because of a patent or because of barriers to entry. Similarly, sentence A might be thought extreme: monopolies, near-monopolies and dominant-firm oligopolies *do* exist, and may survive for a long time before anyone is able to invent and commercialize a new competitive technology. On the other hand, many business people and economists have put forward versions of sentence B and part-sentence C in opposition to government anti-trust or anti-monopoly legislation.

This discussion could be expanded into a **writing** exercise by asking learners to write a paragraph of about 150–200 words beginning:

either

'Monopolies and market concentration should always be forbidden because …'

or

'Monopolies can sometimes be justified because …'

New words in this unit

barriers to entry	monopolistic
cartel	competition
dominant-firm	monopoly
oligopoly	monopsony
entrepreneur	natural monopoly
marginal cost	oligopoly
market challenger	patent
market concentration	product
market follower	differentiation
market leader	unique selling
market structure	proposition

Unit 19 | Takeovers, mergers and buyouts

Successful companies, by definition, make a lot of money, which sooner or later has to be spent. One possibility is to invest it all in research and development, but if this is successful it eventually leads to even greater cash returns. Another possibility is to spend the money by acquiring other companies, whether suppliers, distributors, competitors, or companies in unrelated fields (which again, if successful, eventually leads to even greater cash returns). This unit discusses the ways in which mergers and friendly and hostile takeovers take place, and the advantages and disadvantages of growth by way of mergers and acquisitions. There is also a text about leveraged buyouts, which often result in large conglomerates being split up again, and a writing exercise, practising connectors, concerning the Vodafone/Mannesmann takeover.

1 Mergers and acquisitions

The **cartoon** reflects a widespread belief – and perhaps a reality – that company directors often acquire other companies primarily to satisfy their own egos or predatory instincts. This may be worth discussing.

1a Vocabulary

This exercise introduces the basic vocabulary necessary to discuss mergers and acquisitions.

> ### ANSWERS
>
> **1** to innovate (innovation)   **2** to diversify (diversification)   **3** to merge (a merger)
> **4** a raid   **5** a takeover bid   **6** horizontal integration   **7** vertical integration
> **8** backward integration   **9** forward integration   **10** synergy

Vocabulary note The noun *takeover* is one word but the verb *take over* is two.

1b Discussion

> ### ANSWERS
>
> Oil companies tend to be vertically integrated, owning (or leasing) the oil-wells, and owning their own refineries and petrol (GB) or gas (US) stations. Some electricity companies own their own power stations (though they tend to buy fuel, whether oil, coal or uranium), and provide the cables that go to the homes and business premises of individual consumers; in other countries electricity generators and distributors are separated by law. Water companies do not usually own rivers, but usually have their own reservoirs, and run the pipes to consumers. Car makers usually have networks of franchised dealers, which means that they do not actually *own* them. They generally get their components from a large number of subcontractors. The same applies to the companies that build (or assemble) bicycles, radios and televisions. Some furniture manufacturers have their own stores, but they do not own the forests where the wood comes from. Food companies rarely own their own land or animals, or shops. Newspapers do not grow their own trees for paper, or own the outlets that sell their product.

1c Discussion

> ### ANSWERS
>
> **1** A or B (B, if you believe that top executives are important to a company, or A, if the reason behind the takeover is precisely to get rid of bad managers)

There are obviously no definitive right or wrong answers for the most and least persuasive arguments. Here, however, are a few remarks.

Number 11 appears to be a solid reason in favour of growth, whereas although number 14 may be true, an inefficient company is soon likely to find new competitors entering the market. Of the negative arguments, although 15 may be true, it does not invalidate number 9. Number 1 is a common argument – see, e.g. Thomas J. Peters and Robert H. Waterman: *In Search of Excellence: Lessons from America's Best-Run Companies* (New York: Harper and Row, 1982) – but there is more to a company than top managers and capital equipment: a taken-over company may also have a skilled work force, successful brands, a good reputation, a lot of goodwill, and so on. Number 5 also comes from Peters and Waterman. Number 13 is a key argument of Michael Porter in two well-known and well-received books, *Competitive Strategy* (New York: Free Press, 1980), and *Competitive Advantage* (New York: Free Press, 1985).

1d Listening 🔊

TAPESCRIPT

Interviewer Mr Pocock, could you just tell me a little about the history of Cambridge Instruments?

Max Pocock Cambridge Instruments was formed more than a hundred years ago. It had a reputation for craftsmanship, for quality, but primarily serving the needs of the local university. As the business grew it got very much involved in, in much more the high-tech end of products, it produced the world's first scanning electron microscope. Pushing back the frontiers brought about some problems. Perhaps the company was not focused enough on profits, and in fact in the late 70s the company was taken into public ownership. With Margaret Thatcher coming to power, the company came out of public ownership, was acquired by an entrepreneur and the company went through a very rapid period of growth. In 1990 Cambridge Instruments then merged with Wild-Leitz and the international corporation now known as Leica was formed.

English for Business Studies Second Edition
© Cambridge University Press 2002

ANSWERS

Note Although the *company* called Leica was only formed in 1990, the German company Wild-Leitz had previously used the name 'Leica' as a brand name for its cameras.

1e Listening 🔊

TAPESCRIPT

Interviewer And this was definitely a merger rather than a takeover?

Max Pocock I think very much it *was* a merger. In numbers of employees perhaps the Wild-Leitz was six or seven thousand people and the Cambridge Instruments was three or four thousand, but in terms of profitability of Cambridge Instruments was greater than that of Wild-Leitz so I think it was very much a partnership of two equals.

Interviewer So what exactly was the purpose of the merger, of forming this partnership?

Max Pocock I think the prime purpose of the merger was we had two European companies but neither of whom were world players. We were major European players. This particular market that we're now in is very much dominated by Japanese companies like Hitachi. The feeling was that individually neither company would be able to tackle or take on or match the performance of the Japanese companies, whereas together…and in fact the mission of the Leica Corporation now is to be the world's first choice provider.

Interviewer And you've succeeded?

Max Pocock Without any doubt, I think it's been a success. If I was an accountant, look at the numbers, it is a success, but I think also in a wider sense the customer base has grown, the products are much better, the services to the customers are much better.

English for Business Studies Second Edition
© Cambridge University Press 2002

POSSIBLE ANSWERS

1 Wild-Leitz was a larger company with more employees, but Cambridge Instruments was more profitable.

2 The purpose of the merger was to become 'a world player', large enough to compete with Hitachi and other Japanese companies, and become the most successful company in the industry.

3 He mentions the numbers or figures to be found in the accounts, e.g. turnover and profits, the increase in the number of customers they serve (the customer base), the improvement of the products, and the improvement of customer service.

Note Both Max Pocock and the interviewer talk about the 'partnership' between the merged companies Wild-Leitz and Cambridge Instruments. This just means two groups of formerly separate people working together, and not a partnership in the *legal* sense (a form of unincorporated business enterprise in which all the partners have unlimited liability).

1f Listening 🔊

TAPESCRIPT

Interviewer What about on the human level? How did the people in the two companies react to the merger?

Max Pocock There was a lot of coming together very very early on of a lot of people. Because both companies are pushing back the frontiers of technology there's an immediate common interest in each other's technology. Probably, in many areas, this was two companies who had until the day before had been competing, who until the day before had been trying very hard to find out what each other was up to, what each was doing, how their things worked, suddenly for all these technical people all the answers were all there so that probably, that very early sharing of technology probably helped to allay an awful lot, an awful lot of fears but there were, there were areas and there were countries, for example, where each of the parties had, for example, a sales unit where these were merged and there were people who lost their jobs but they were done as sympathetically as can be done, there was nobody who was put out on the street at a day's notice with no compensation.

Interviewer Were there any other consequences of this merger that you haven't mentioned?

Max Pocock For many of us the coming together of the two companies brought about the need for changes as well and this is now where Leica will be like a great majority of companies in the last years, as we become more and more customer focused, all the things about outsourcing, rightsizing, all of these things, they're just as common within Leica, we're probably much better capable and able to deal with them because of the size, and our position in the market.

English for Business Studies Second Edition
© Cambridge University Press 2002

1 The technical staff in both companies were interested in finding out about each other's advanced technology, and in sharing it.

2 The staff in each company had been trying very hard to discover what the other one was planning, doing and making, and how its products worked.

3 In the sales units in some countries (as the company formed by the merger required fewer sales staff).

4 He mentions outsourcing and rightsizing. Outsourcing means contracting out work (the construction of components, the supply of various services, and so on) to outside companies, which inevitably leads to the company itself employing fewer staff. Rightsizing also means making sure that the company has the right number of staff to be optimally profitable, which again generally leads to the company employing fewer staff.

2 Buyouts

2a Reading

ANSWERS

Most of the following sentences and part-sentences should be underlined:

- … many of these conglomerates consisted of too many companies and not enough synergy. After the recession of the early 1980s, there were many large companies on the US stock market with good earnings but low stock prices. Their assets were worth more than the companies' market value. *(lines 5–8)*

- Such conglomerates were clearly not maximizing stockholder value. The individual companies might have been more efficient if liberated from central management. Consequently, raiders were able to borrow money, buy badly-managed, inefficient and underpriced corporations, and then restructure them, split them up, and resell them at a profit. *(lines 9–13)*

- Although the market could understand data concerning companies' earnings, it was highly inefficient in valuing assets, including land, buildings and pension funds. Asset-stripping – selling off the assets of poorly performing or under-valued companies – proved to be highly lucrative. *(lines 16–19)*

- Theoretically, there was little risk of making a loss with a buyout, as the debts incurred were guaranteed by the companies' assets. *(lines 20–21)*

- … the high returns on debt issued by risky enterprises more than compensated for their riskiness, as the rate of default was lower than might be expected. *(lines 29–31)*

- … the permanent threat of takeovers is a challenge to company managers and directors to do their jobs better, and … well-run businesses that are not undervalued are at little risk. The threat of raids forces companies to put capital to productive use. Fat or lazy companies that fail to do this will be taken over by raiders who will use assets more efficiently, cut costs, and increase shareholder value. *(lines 35–39)*

2b Summarizing

Learners can be asked to complete these sentences either verbally (working in pairs), or in writing (alone or working in pairs).

TYPICAL ANSWERS

1 The fact that many large conglomerates' assets were worth more than their stock market valuation demonstrated that they were clearly not maximizing stockholder value, i.e. giving their stockholders the maximum possible return on their investment.

2 Raiders bought conglomerates in order to strip them of their assets, i.e. to restructure them, split them up, and resell the pieces at a profit.

3 Raiders showed that the stock market did not necessarily value companies' assets correctly, especially land, buildings and pension funds.

4 Raiders were particularly interested in companies with large cash reserves, companies with successful subsidiaries that could be sold, and companies in fields that are not sensitive to a recession.

5 Investors were prepared to lend money to finance LBOs because they received a high rate of interest which more than compensated for the risk that the bonds would not be repaid.

6 Raiders argue that the possibility of a buyout forces company managers and directors to do their jobs well, and to use their capital productively.

2c Writing

ANSWERS

1 for example   2 Furthermore   3 Yet
4 in other words   5 on the contrary
6 Moreover   7 for instance   8 Even though
9 i.e.   10 however   11 Nevertheless
12 Although   13 because   14 Consequently

2d Discussion

There are clearly no right answers as to which arguments are the most persuasive.

See also the role plays 'Who should we take over?' and 'Integration' in *Business Roles* by John Crowther-Alwyn (Cambridge University Press).

New words in this unit

arbitrageur	management buyout
asset-stripping	or MBO
backward integration	raid
competitive advantage	raider
diversification	recession
forward integration	stockholder value
horizontal integration	synergy
hostile takeover	takeover bid
leveraged buyout or	vertical integration
LBO	

Test 3 | Finance

Part One: Vocabulary

Write the words or expressions defined in the sentences in the boxes on page 100.

(7 means one word of seven letters; 4,4 means two words of four letters, and so on.)

 1 A person in possession of privileged financial information (7).

 2 A security in a large, safe, profitable company (4,4).

 3 Describes the price of a bond trading at over 100% (5,3).

 4 A loan to buy property or real estate, with the property (house, apartment, etc.) serving as a guarantee for the loan (8).

 5 To fail to pay back a loan (7).

 6 A bond that pays variable interest according to market conditions (8,4,4).

 7 To end the activities of a bankrupt company (4,2).

 8 Describes stock exchanges for newer and smaller companies (4,3,7).

 9 A company's proportion of bonds to stocks (4,6,5).

10 The date at which a loan will be repaid (8).

11 The return produced by an investment (5).

12 A wholesaler in stocks who deals with stockbrokers (6,5).

13 A long-term note issued by the US government, to borrow money (8,4).

14 A stock that is expected to give a good return but not fluctuate in price (9,5).

15 The name given to the fiscal advantage of issuing bonds rather than stocks (3,6).

16 A bond that can be exchanged for stock, under certain conditions (11,4).

17 To issue shares to the public for the first time (5).

18 One of several names for new shares distributed to shareholders instead of a dividend (5,5).

19 The nominal rate of interest on a fixed-interest stock (6).

20 To sell a bankrupt company's assets to repay creditors (9).

21 The amount of a loan, paid back at maturity (9).

22 New shares offered at below their nominal value to existing shareholders (6,5).

English for Business Studies Second Edition
© Cambridge University Press 2002

Debt and equity financing

1   D
2   E
3   B
4   T
5   A
6   N
7   D
8   E
9   Q
10   U
11   I
12   T
13   Y
14   F
15   I
16   N
17   A
18   N
19   C
20   I
21   N
22   G

English for Business Studies Second Edition
© Cambridge University Press 2002

Part Two: Speaking

Allocate each learner one of the following subjects, to speak about for *two minutes*, after ten minutes of preparation with the Student's Book and their course notes.

1 What information is usually included in a balance sheet?
2 What is the difference between commercial and investment banks?
3 What are the legal requirements of companies which issue stocks or shares?
4 What are the advantages and disadvantages of issuing bonds?
5 What causes the price of bonds to fluctuate?
6 Why do futures markets exist?
7 What are derivatives?
8 What are the two main ways in which a company can acquire another company?
9 Why is it sometimes possible to make a profit out of a leveraged buyout?

Part Three: Composition

Possible composition titles:

1 Why do virtually all companies finance themselves with a mixture of debt and equity?
2 Is it now possible for companies to manage *all* financial risks with derivatives (futures, options, swaps, etc.)?
3 Should there be laws to prevent large companies getting an ever-increasing market share?
4 What is the logic behind growth by takeovers, and is it necessarily a good one?
5 Any publicly-quoted company in Britain or America can at any time be the target of a hostile takeover bid or raid. Is this a desirable state of affairs?

ANSWERS

Part One: Vocabulary

1	I N S I **D** E R
2	B L U **E** C H I P
3	A **B** O V E P A R
4	M O R **T** G A G E
5	D E F **A** U L T
6	F L O A T I **N** G R A T E N O T E
7	W I N **D** U P
8	O V E R T H **E** C O U N T E R
9	D E B T E **Q** U I T Y R A T I O
10	M A T **U** R I T Y
11	Y **I** E L D
12	M A R K E **T** M A K E R
13	T R E A S U R **Y** B O N D
14	D E **F** E N S I V E S T O C K
15	T A X S H **I** E L D
16	C O **N** V E R T I B L E B O N D
17	F L O **A** T
18	B O **N** U S I S S U E
19	**C** O U P O N
20	L I Q U **I** D A T E
21	P R I **N** C I P A L
22	R I **G** H T S I S S U E

English for Business Studies Second Edition
© Cambridge University Press 2002

Unit 20 | Efficiency and employment

Since the beginning of the 1980s, the world has seen enormous economic changes. In the industrialized countries, financial markets were deregulated, leading to an integrated global financial system without restrictions on capital flows. Many formerly nationalized industries were privatized. Advances in computer technology led to considerable structural changes. The newly industrialized countries in Asia continued to grow and to export. In 1989, the 'Iron Curtain' dividing Europe disappeared, and the formerly communist regimes in Central and Eastern Europe began their transition to market economies. Faced with global competition, many companies felt the need to become more efficient, which is often another way of saying they need to employ fewer people. Unemployment has grown rapidly throughout Europe.

This unit contains an interview with an economist who suggests what changes will have to be made if job security continues to decrease and labour markets become more flexible, and an article disputing the common conception that we are living in a period of increased job insecurity.

1 Labour market flexibility

1a Vocabulary and discussion

There are clearly no 'right answers' here, but there are several obvious discussion points.

Computerization and *technology* clearly have advantages. For example, most language learners today are too young to remember the days before cash dispensers, when many people had to remember to go to the bank on Friday, otherwise they'd have no money for the weekend. But computerization is probably destroying more jobs (bank employees, secretaries, etc.) than it has created so far.

Productivity is obviously important, as increased productivity is the only source of increased wealth, but, on the other hand, *rationalization*, *flexibility* and *restructuring* can all lead to unemployment. Many economists argue that *deregulation* enables markets to work more efficiently, but it can also lead to a loss of jobs or job security.

Decentralization means delegating responsibilities to local subsidiaries, etc., rather than controlling everything from a central headquarters. This was discussed in Unit 5. (Decentralization is not to be confused with delocalization, the moving of production units, etc. to cheaper countries.)

Some people, especially those of an entrepreneurial nature, want to work for themselves. Others equate *self-employment* with long hours and a lack of advantages such as sick pay, holiday pay, and so on. Some people advocate *job-sharing* as a solution to unemployment, others do not believe that jobs with responsibilities can be shared. (Note: job-sharing – two people sharing the same post – is not to be confused with the division of labour – the specialization of work discussed long ago by Adam Smith in *The Wealth of Nations*.)

A lot of people believe in *public services* (health, education, transport, etc.), although they often dislike paying the *taxes* that make them possible. Others dislike public services because they believe that the size of the government or the state should be diminished, and because they are frequently inefficient, as they are not subject to competition. *Welfare* has two meanings – general well-being (health, happiness, prosperity, and so on), and also financial assistance given to people in need (also called social security). Most people are in favour of the former; some people disapprove of the latter.

Political *stability* is generally thought to be a good thing, but economic change is usually inevitable. *Structural change* (or what the Austrian economist

Joseph Schumpeter called 'creative destruction') often leads to growth and the development of new industries, but obviously causes problems for declining industries. The advantages and disadvantages of *free trade* and *globalization* are discussed in Unit 27. Economic *growth* is mentioned in relation to pollution in Unit 28.

1b Discussion

Learners are likely to have enough knowledge of these matters to allow a short discussion, before the reading and listening activities devoted to this topic.

1c Listening 🔊

Note Kate Barker speaks very quickly in this extract; it will probably be necessary to play each section three times.

TAPESCRIPT

Kate Barker In Britain, in the period of the 1980s and early 1990s, the Conservative Party pursued a deliberate policy of making labour markets very much more flexible. This meant that it's easier to bring people into the labour market, because companies are less worried about the costs of having to make them redundant subsequently. And this had a number of advantages. It's particularly considered to have encouraged inward investment, especially from the Japanese, because they didn't think they were going to get stuck with very high labour costs if the demand that they were expecting for their products wasn't quite fulfilled. However in terms…, while it's been very good for companies, because it's made it easier for company managements to keep their labour force exactly matched to the levels of demand they're experiencing, it's had a number of drawbacks in terms of public policy.

In particular, the structure of unemployment benefits needs to be revisited if you have people moving between employment and unemployment much more quickly. The structure of pensions needs to be revisited if you have people no longer working for a long time for the same employer, and finally in Britain we tend to have a very high level of owner-occupation – more people own their own homes, and they borrow a great deal of money in order to pay for that. That's a very difficult thing to do if you're moving in and out of two to three year, two to three year contracts. It would be much more logical to have a big private rented sector if you want to have a very flexible labour market, and actually it's not just flexible in the sense that people change their jobs, but they may actually change where they live, and again that's very difficult to do if you actually own your own home.

English for Business Studies Second Edition
© Cambridge University Press 2002

ANSWERS

1 B
2 They can hire and fire workers quite easily, according to changes in demand for their products or services.
3 Foreign investors, such as Japanese companies, were encouraged to open factories in Britain, because they knew that it would be easier and cheaper to make workers redundant if they were no longer wanted.
4 1 unemployment benefits   2 pensions
   3 own their own homes   4 private rented sector

1d Comprehension 🔊

TAPESCRIPT

Kate Barker The United States has historically also had a much more flexible market than the European, than the European Community. It's therefore had the same effects that it has in Britain whereby there have been the

---

growth of people who are long-term unemployed, but also the fact that when you, that employment has adjusted very quickly. In downturns employment falls very fast, but in an upturn employment rises more quickly, the labour market has been taken back into employment more readily. But again that's because people think they can make their employees redundant more quickly. But, one of the costs of it is that these people who are brought back into employment when the economy is growing more strongly tend to be brought back in at really rather low wage levels, and in both Britain and the United States there's been a tremendous growth in inequality, so that the gap between the top 10% of earners and the bottom 10% of earners has tended to widen, and that's now leading to social problems which is a cause of concern in both countries.

One of the problems that's arisen in Britain and also in the United States, is that with these more flexible labour markets, and with the pressures from global competition, with the fact that we now have a lot more pressure from very low wage markets in South East Asia, and also from the more developing parts of the world, we've had the development of a sort of underclass of worker. These are the people who get brought in when the economy is very close to capacity, and they're often brought in at relatively low wages, and they're the people who go out, who go out most quickly, and their sort of hold in society is therefore very much more transitory. It's very much more difficult for them to maintain their place in society. And it's among this group that there's a great risk that social unrest can develop. We've seen evidence from this in terms of difficulties in higher, in much higher rates of crime in areas of high unemployment, and that's been quite evident in Britain and to a lesser extent in the United States.

English for Business Studies Second Edition
© Cambridge University Press 2002

ANSWERS

1 B (Kate Barker says *employment* falls in a downturn; this must not be confused with the negative *unemployment*.)

2 B ('in an upturn employment rises more quickly … But again that's because people think that they can make their employees redundant more quickly')

3 A ('these people who are brought back into employment when the economy is growing more strongly tend to be brought back in at really rather low wage levels')

4 C ('we now have a lot more pressure from very low wage markets in South East Asia')

1e Listening 🔊

TAPESCRIPT

Kate Barker If you're interested in trying to deal with the problem of poverty, and the problem of people being kept out of work, there are a number of measures that the government, that governments can take. A very obvious measure is to try and make sure that people who are unemployed are given, offered a relatively good level of training, so that they are made a bit more attractive to employers. Other measures that governments have tried to use, particularly in Britain, is to offer employers who take on long-term unemployed reductions in social security benefits, the costs, the extra costs that employers have to meet in terms of social security contributions, so that they, so that it is actually cheaper for them for the first six months or so to take on somebody who's long-term unemployed, and one of the benefits of this is that it may help employers to reassess their attitude towards people who have been out of work for a long time, who historically they've tended to think of as rather second-class, in the employment market.

English for Business Studies Second Edition
© Cambridge University Press 2002

ANSWERS

1 A 'relatively good level of training' for unemployed people, and offering employers reductions in social security contributions for six months if they hire people who have been unemployed for a long time.

2 She says that employers tend to think of the long-term unemployed as rather second-class employees, i.e. to distrust them.

2 Job security

2a Vocabulary

ANSWERS

1 *Employ*: appoint, engage, hire, take on
   Dismiss: fire, lay off, make redundant, sack

2 1 G 2 H 3 F 4 A 5 D 6 E 7 C 8 B

2b Reading

The (shortened and very slightly adapted) article is from the *Financial Times*, 25 January 2001.

ANSWER

The article's sub-title was (b). Both (a) and (c) are mentioned in the article, but are not the main topic.

2c Comprehension

ANSWERS

1 Politicians and journalists, recruitment agencies and management consultants continue to make the flesh creep

2 the supposed world of stable, long-tenured employment that dominated the industrialized economies for the first three decades after the second world war

3 certain sub-groups of the population, such as those with less education, experienced less job security than in the past

4 average job tenure is declining in upswings

5 average job tenure is … increasing in downturns
   (This contradicts Kate Barker's conventional account of why unemployment rises in a recession, and the logic of this argument is not immediately clear.)

6 The decline in job tenure observed in recent years may mainly reflect the economic recovery that has taken place in some countries

7 People working in larger companies are more likely to stay with their employer for a long time

8 a tendency for younger and older workers to have lower retention rates compared with those of prime age

9 we experienced a significant net increase in the amount of temporary work (fixed-term contracts and temporary agency employment)

10 an involuntary loss of work now covers the articulate, skilled white-collar elites

2d Discussion

Arguments *against* some of these suggestions include the following:

● People in boring jobs would probably be happy with a cut in working hours, but not with the consequent reduction of income.

● Retiring at a younger age, or working fewer years in one's life, perhaps taking some years off, for example when your children are young, as many women already do, equally require a reduction of income.

● People with interesting and responsible jobs are often opposed to sharing them with someone else. For example, if you are a brand manager, or the person responsible for dealing with particular clients, investors, or investments, you probably don't want to spend Thursday and Friday at home worrying about what someone else is doing with 'your' job. It is also more expensive for companies to hire two part-time workers for the same job.

- Training programmes are presumably a good idea if there are jobs available that require trained workers, but some unemployed people have few skills and lack the capacities to learn others.
- Public sector jobs obviously have to be paid for out of tax revenue.

The material in this unit lends itself to an additional **writing** exercise: a short composition about 'The advantages and disadvantages of flexible labour markets', or 'Ways of reducing unemployment'.

See also the role plays 'Downsizing' and 'Selling off a line of business' in *Business Roles 2* by John Crowther-Alwyn (Cambridge University Press).

New words in this unit

appoint	lay off
business cycle	make redundant
efficiency	restructuring
employability	sack
engage	self-employment
fire	temporary work
growth	tenure
hire	upswing
job instability	upturn
job-sharing	welfare
labour market flexibility	

Unit 21 | Business ethics

Some people argue that the objective of business, and consequently the role of managers, is to make as much money as possible for companies' owners, the stockholders or shareholders. Other people argue that companies have to be careful never to cheat customers, but for purely business reasons, rather than ethical ones: disappointed customers will not buy any more of your products in future. Still other people insist that companies have social and ethical responsibilities to their customers, their staff, their business partners, their local community, society in general, and the natural environment, that are as important as, or more important than, their responsibility to provide a financial return to their shareholders. This unit includes a text containing opposing views of the social responsibilities of business, and discussion activities concerning the ethics of certain existing business practices.

1 The social responsibility of business

1a Discussion

A good way to introduce this topic, before even looking at **1a**, would be to refer to – or better still, to elicit from the learners – recent news stories relating to ethical or unethical behaviour by well-known companies.

The second view – *caveat emptor* – clearly contradicts modern marketing theory, and the logic of satisfying needs, and of making a long-term customer rather than a single sale.

The fourth and fifth views leave open the question for multinational companies as to *which* laws or conventional standards of morality are applicable to subsidiaries – those of the local country, or those of the country in which the company's headquarters are situated? For example, should foreign companies with subsidiaries in South Africa during the *apartheid* period have followed local customs?

The sixth view clearly leaves the way open for a conflict between the individual employee and the employer's expectations or requirements – although of course it is possible that an employee could have as a personal ethical standard 'business is business' and the employer something more 'social'.

The seventh view – referred to in **1b** as the *stakeholder model*, clearly conflicts with view number three, the *stockholder model*, which is in fact dominant in many countries.

This section draws on an exercise in *An Introduction to Business Ethics*, by George D. Chryssides and John H. Kaler (London: Chapman and Hall, 1993).

1b Reading

> ### ANSWER
>
> Views 3, 4 and 5 are all expressed in the quotation from Milton Friedman. ('Ethical customs' means much the same thing as 'conventional standards of morality'.) View 7 is expressed in the final paragraph.

Friedman's article is reprinted in Chryssides and Kaler's book. He expresses similar views at greater length in *Capitalism and Freedom* (Chicago: University of Chicago Press, 1962).

Vocabulary note French, Italian and Spanish speakers often need to be reminded that *society* in English does *not* mean a company or corporation, but only a large community of people, or a *non-commercial* association.

1c Comprehension

1d Vocabulary

2 Ethics and the law

2a Discussion

As usual, this activity is best done in pairs or small groups, after which the answers can be discussed with the whole class.

There are clearly no definitive 'right' answers to these questions.

Some notes

1 Some people argue that where it is necessary to pay (i.e. bribe) someone to undertake some administrative work, or to do it more quickly, this is equivalent to paying for a service, and is not the same as bribing people in order to win business contracts. But how should such payments be entered in the company's accounts?

2 It has been suggested – provocatively, and probably not entirely seriously – that industrial espionage is merely a continuation of the logic of *benchmarking*, which means going outside the company to discover the best practices in an industry, and copying them!

3 Like the concept *caveat emptor*, built-in obsolescence again clearly conflicts with the modern marketing concept of satisfying faithful customers. However, if products last too long…

4 Some people have gone as far as describing political power (a consequence of lobbying) as 'the fifth P of marketing'.

5 Most countries have legislation concerning seriously misleading advertising. The same objection can be made to telling only half the truth, or exaggerating a great deal, or keeping quiet about bad aspects of products in advertising as can be made to built-in obsolescence: it conflicts with the marketing logic of creating long-term customers. Yet the advertising for products that people pay for only once will always tend to exaggerate, e.g. people are unlikely to stop going to the cinema because they dislike one misleadingly-advertised movie. And chocolate manufacturers, for example, are unlikely to mention in their advertising that their product is probably bad for your teeth, your weight, and your skin complexion.

6 In countries such as Switzerland, which allow 'hidden reserves', profit smoothing is generally considered to be acceptable, so auditors will not complain, and need not be threatened. Many people defend this system, comparing it favourably to the short-term thinking prevalent in the United States, where many companies publish quarterly profit figures.

7 Whistle-blowers are likely to be dismissed for breach of contract. One question which often arises is whether they deserve legal protection or compensation.

On the next page is an additional, photocopiable case study.

Business ethics: A case study

In the summer of 1995, Barclays Bank spent £180 million of its profits in buying back shares from its shareholders. In the preceding years, many other companies in America and Britain had done the same thing, among them IBM, Philip Morris, PepsiCo, Merck, Boots and Reuters. This is a way of boosting share prices and earnings per share, but it also shows that these companies cannot find projects to invest their money in, and demonstrates that they are making excessive profits. According to economic theory, companies making excessive returns in an efficient market will find competitors entering their industry until profits return to normal. The fact that this has not happened shows that the industries affected by the buy-back phenomenon must be operating more like *de facto* cartels than free competitive markets.

The big institutional shareholders (insurance companies and pension funds) probably prefer to sell their shares back to companies, rather than see these companies spend their money on doubtful takeovers. But they want to reinvest this money in other blue chip companies, rather than in riskier smaller businesses. Clearly if all big companies stop investing and start buying back their shares there will be a problem.

If a company's guiding objective is to 'increase shareholder value', buying back shares with excess profits is the only logical thing to do. If this should *not* be a company's basic objective, other alternatives are possible. For example, Barclays Bank could have:

- re-employed some of the 20,000 people it had dismissed from their jobs in the previous four years in order to reduce costs
- increased the salaries of its remaining 95,000 staff
- offered lower prices (fees and commissions) to its customers
- negotiated higher prices with its suppliers
- written off a large part of its loans to Third World countries that are unable to repay them
- used the money in other ways, according to the argument that companies have responsibilities to the community in which they operate

If it were your decision, would you buy back the shares, or choose other alternatives to spend Barclays' £180 million profits?

English for Business Studies Second Edition
© Cambridge University Press 2002

Notes Many businesses argue that it is necessary to cut staffing costs in order to be competitive, but a bank that has £180 million in profits that it doesn't know what to do with is clearly competitive. Yet if it is functioning efficiently with recently reduced staffing levels, it is unlikely to see the need to hire more people. A bank making high profits must also have a large number of customers who are sufficiently satisfied to stay with the bank and not move to a competitor, so it is unlikely to want to offer lower prices. Similarly, it is unlikely to want to increase salaries or the prices it pays to suppliers to anything above the 'market price' in the banking industry. The idea of a bank in some way 'giving' £180 million to the community in which it operates also seems implausible. Many people would argue that there are important humanitarian reasons for Western banks to write off their loans to developing African countries, which have far lower levels of income, education spending and health care, and far higher levels of poverty and infant mortality than a generation ago. This argument, however, is not one that has convinced many banks.

Consequently, the trend of large companies buying back some of their equities seems likely to continue.

See also the role play 'Polluting the river' in *Business Roles* by John Crowther-Alwyn, and the simulations 'Smoke signals', 'A pirate's dilemma', and 'Dirty work' in *Decisionmaker* by David Evans (Cambridge University Press).

New words in this unit

bribery	pollution
built-in obsolescence	social responsibility
ethics	stakeholder
industrial espionage	welfare capitalism
lobbying	whistle blowing
perfect competition	

Unit 22 | The role of government

For the past two or three decades, determining the role of the government has perhaps been *the* central political and economic issue in industrialized democracies. Although the number of nationalized (government-owned) industries is steadily declining in most parts of the world, people with left-wing views still generally believe that the government has an essential role to play in providing the economic infrastructure (public transport, telecommunications, and so on) and ensuring the provision of services such as education, health care, social security and perhaps housing, and regulating working conditions, health and safety standards, and so on. People with right-wing views, on the contrary, generally argue that many (or most, or maybe all) of these activities can be left to private enterprise and the market system, and that the role of the government should perhaps be restricted to activities such as defence, the police, and the justice system. They argue that too much regulation is bad for business, and leads to inefficiency. This is an argument that is *not* going to go away.

Subsequent units deal with central banking, monetary policy, taxation, and the role of the government in the business cycle. This unit deals more generally with the responsibilities of government, offering two contrasting perspectives from well-known American economists, and also with the relationship between government and industry, especially in relation to the promotion of exports.

1 What are governments for?

Discussion

Most people appear to be confident that the political views they hold at any particular moment are right – perhaps teachers even more so than their younger business students – but political propaganda has not been proved to facilitate the acquisition of foreign languages. (In other words, one should always try hard *not* to interrupt or ridicule language learners who put forward ideas with which one strongly disagrees, as could happen here.)

2 Two views of the role of government

2a Reading

> **ANSWER**
>
> Galbraith mentions parks and recreational facilities, libraries, the arts, supporting science and medical research, and investing in and regulating the environment.

2b Comprehension

> **ANSWERS**
>
> 1 Galbraith points out that they usually have enough money to provide these services for themselves, whereas there are other people who do not.
> 2 Galbraith talks of the limited time horizons of the market economy, meaning that it usually requires a rapid return on investments, and so will not invest in scientific research that has no short-term profit potential.
> 3 Galbraith is clearly what in Europe would be called a social democrat, and in the USA, a liberal.

Vocabulary note *Liberal* is a very problematic word, which means different things to different people. For *Americans*, a liberal is someone (like Galbraith, or Democrat Presidents such as Kennedy and Clinton) who believes in state intervention in the economy. (The opposite, which applies to recent Republican Presidents, is *conservative*.)

But in *Britain*, the Liberals were for many years the centre party, between Labour (socialist or social democrat) and the Conservatives. Consequently in Britain, a liberal is someone who is neither on the left nor right. In common British usage, Galbraith would probably be described as a social democrat.

Yet in pure economic terms, dating from the early 19th century, *liberal* denotes a belief in free markets, without governmental intervention, and is thus part of the name of right-wing political parties in many European countries and languages, for whom Milton Friedman, who has entirely contrary views to Galbraith, would be an excellent example of a liberal, or what today is often called a neo-liberal.

2c Vocabulary

ANSWERS

1 evident   2 low-cost   3 at odds with
4 illness   5 borne in mind (to bear in mind)
6 the underclass   7 the affluent
8 achievements   9 reluctantly
10 planetary

2d Reading

ANSWER

According to the Friedmans, the role of the government has expanded far too much. Its interventions in the economy might even end economic progress. The government severely limits people's freedom to spend their money and work as they choose. We need to end a lot of existing restrictions.

2e Comprehension

ANSWERS

1 'Currently, more than 40% of our income is disposed of on our behalf by government at federal, state and local levels combined.'

2 They disapprove of the law that makes it compulsory to fix seat belts to cars. (When *Free to Choose* was written, it was not yet compulsory in the USA to *use* the seat belts fitted in cars.)

3 That all business activities and transactions are voluntary, and nobody uses force or coercion.

4 They disapprove of the necessity of doctors (physicians) and dentists requiring a government-controlled permit or a licence before they can go into business, and they regret that doctors are not free to choose which drugs or medicines to prescribe, but must obey laws and restrictions that are sometimes unique to the USA.

5 They believe that workers should be free to work any number of hours they agree with their employer, without restrictions imposed by the government.

6 The Friedmans clearly believe in free markets and few governmental restrictions. They are probably best described as right-wing libertarian. (But see **2b** above.)

2f Vocabulary

ANSWERS

1 C	2 H	3 D	4 B	5 E
6 I	7 J	8 F	9 G	10 A

Vocabulary note The Friedman text uses the American words *automobile* and *railroad*; the British say *car* and *railway*. Similarly, Americans use *truck* and *airplane*, while the British say *lorry* and *aeroplane*. The text uses the word *physician*; the British usually talk about a *doctor*. It also uses the American word *mortician* (a person who prepares the dead for burial or cremation, and arranges funerals). The British equivalent is *undertaker*. But, of course, the verb *to undertake* means to promise to do something. Undertaker is *not* another word for entrepreneur.

2g Discussion

The answer to the second question is no, not explicitly. Galbraith mentions low-cost housing, health care, parks, recreational facilities, police, libraries, the arts, scientific research and the environment. The Friedmans do not specifically mention any of these areas, apart from their comments on physicians, but it is clear that they do not want to pay all the taxes (to have the government dispose of a large part of their income) necessary to support these activities.

An additional **writing** exercise would be to summarize Galbraith's and the Friedmans' views of the role of government in a couple of paragraphs (which would involve expanding the answer given in **2d**). The paragraphs could include the following expressions:

> J. K. Galbraith believes that it is the role of the state to …
> … because the market system …
> Milton and Rose Friedman, on the contrary …
> They regret that we are not free to …

3 Government and industry

3a Discussion

There is clearly no right answer to this question, although most advanced countries *do* make great efforts to increase their exports. There is often a government department that can give information and other help to exporting countries (which is discussed in the listening activity below); 'aid' given to poorer countries sometimes consists of goods manufactured in the rich country itself; and at least since the end of the 'cold war' (the destruction of the Berlin Wall and the dissolution of the Soviet Union), there have been lots of stories about the security services of Western countries spying on industries in rival countries, and doing whatever necessary to ensure that manufacturers in their countries succeed in getting large export contracts.

3b Listening 🔊

TAPESCRIPT

Julian Amey I'm Julian Amey, working for DTI, in the export promotions side, particularly looking at media, education and training, and telecommunications.

Interviewer In the DTI, how much of the time is spent with exports? Is that the majority of the DTI's work, trying to encourage British exports?

Julian Amey It's one of the three key areas of DTI involvement. Exports and the development of trade and investment is the business of this department of DTI, but the other main areas where the DTI is involved is in terms of developing industry in the UK, making sure that appropriate technologies and investments are forthcoming for key industry areas, and the second area apart from exports has to do with regulation and competition, that's to say ensuring open, competing markets, mergers and monopolies policy, that kind of thing.

Interviewer And what sort of things can the DTI do to encourage investment and trade? What are the general ways in which that's done?

Julian Amey Well, this has been under review for the last three years, given that there is now a philosophy, if you like, that there *is* a role for government although it has to be very carefully tailored to the perceived requirements of industry. That is to say industry itself must have a strong voice in what that help is. And the main focus of DTI's work at the moment is to provide detailed analysis of the markets, the priority

---

markets that Britain is aiming for, for the service of industry, and then help, particularly for the small and medium sized companies, to tackle those markets in an efficient way.

Well, the specific help is that each priority market, there are 80 of them, 80 key markets around the world, have a desk officer who's wholly responsible for providing information about that country, let's say Brazil, so you'll have a Brazil desk officer who can give you all the detailed economic and political information about the market, sector information on whatever interests you, whether it's oil and gas or consumer goods or whatever, and then they can beyond that give you the help of our embassy in Brazil, which itself has commercial officers who can get further information about market segments and, for example, possibly agents which might act for your business.

Small and medium sized companies, by their nature, cannot be expected to have the resource to understand in detail every market where they might be doing business, so we can help those companies in the first steps into a market until they've got the momentum going which carries them forward.

English for Business Studies Second Edition
© Cambridge University Press 2002

ANSWERS

1 The DTI tries to ensure that (a) important sectors of industry in Britain are able to invest in and to benefit from the right technologies, and (b) that markets are open and competitive, which includes ensuring that mergers and takeovers do not prevent competition among firms.

2 B

3 The DTI's most important area of activity is providing detailed analyses of overseas markets, especially for small and medium sized companies wanting to export goods or services.

4 (a) In Britain, the DTI has 80 desk officers, each responsible for providing detailed economic and political information about markets and particular market sectors in a different country; (b) abroad, there are commercial officers working in British embassies, who are able to give further information, and to assist in making contact with local agents.

5 1 key (or priority)   2 appropriate
3 tailored to   4 aiming for   5 tackle
6 agents   7 resource (Note: this word is more commonly used as a plural: *resources*.)

3c Listening 🔊

TAPESCRIPT

Julian Amey … for example, telecommunications, a key area where we are hoping to develop the UK position in many countries around the world. We have a very good industry base, we have major companies involved, fairly obviously Cable and Wireless, British Telecom, and a whole host of others who are providing for the telecoms industry.

Last year we had a company, actually based in Northern Ireland, which wanted to get into the Latin American market, and they had no former connections in the area. They first of all attended a seminar that we ran in Belfast where we briefed industry on the new economic and political situation in Latin America. They decided then that they wanted to visit the markets and so they were able to join a mission which we supported by giving grants, that's to say a travel and accommodation grant which makes it obviously more accessible for a company to enter the market. They went out to the market, found immediately a company that wanted their product and were able to set up a million dollar order on that first visit and from that visit they then established a local representative who is busy developing their market, so that was quite a nice example.

English for Business Studies Second Edition
© Cambridge University Press 2002

New words in this unit

affluent	market forces
health care	poverty
housing	taxpayer
intervention	the state
market economy	underclass

Unit 23 | Central banking, money and taxation

Central banks are responsible for implementing monetary policy, i.e. controlling – or attempting to control – the money supply (and consequently inflation) and interest rates. In some countries, the central bank is independent from the government, in others it is controlled by the government. In the former case, the government will be unable to instigate expansionary policies, either to boost an economy in a recession, or to create a boom before the next election. This unit contains an interview with an economist about the role of central banks and the issue of their independence from government.

Governments that are unable to borrow money, or simply to print it, have to finance their expenditures by raising taxes. This unit also contains a text about the main forms of taxation – and the ways in which tax-payers attempt to avoid paying it – and discussion and writing exercises on the pros and cons of taxation.

1 Central banking

1a Listening 🔊

TAPESCRIPT

Interviewer Gabriel Mangano, you're an expert on central banking. Could you briefly summarize the functions of a central bank?

Gabriel Mangano Yes. I would say there are four of them. The first one is actually to implement monetary policy. There are roughly three ways to do it. First setting interest rate ceilings and floors, which means limiting, upwards or downwards, the fluctuations of the interest rate. The second way to implement monetary policy is simply printing money, or destroying it – coins, banknotes. The third one, which is a bit more modern, is those open-market operations, which are simply buying and selling government bonds to and from commercial banks.

So that was the first main task of a central bank. The second one is exchange rate supervision, I would say. Mainly for floating exchange rates but one should not forget that even for a fixed exchange rate the central bank still has to make sure that it has enough reserves to counteract any upswing or downswing of this exchange rate.

Third main task, yes, commercial banking supervision I would say – make sure that the commercial banks have enough liquidities, for instance, to avoid any bank run.

Interviewer What's a bank run?

Gabriel Mangano The bank run is a sort of, a kind of panic, a situation in which investors or simply customers of the banks run to the bank and take their money out because they realize or they think they realize that their bank is not trustworthy any more. And to avoid this actually, the central bank has to make sure that they have a sufficient liquidity ratio, for instance.

Fourth main task of the central bank would be to act as a lender of last resort in case, actually, one of these commercial banks goes bankrupt and the investors, the people putting money in the bank, have to get back their money.

English for Business Studies Second Edition
© Cambridge University Press 2002

1b Vocabulary

1c Listening 🔊

TAPESCRIPT

Interviewer And I know that you believe that central banks should normally be independent from the government, rather than a government department. Why is this?

Gabriel Mangano Well, the main reason is what we call, in economics, the political business cycle. If the central bank mainly acts as a branch of government, then this government is inclined – incited – to increase abruptly, for instance, money supply just before elections in order to favour employment, but, of course, this has a negative effect on inflation, but as the government is not sure to be re-elected, at least it has some positive impact on employment just before the election, which is positive. There are also other reasons, which are more technical probably, but the main other one I would quote is the fact that it's more efficient for a separate body to implement monetary policy while the government is really only restrained to implementing what we call budgetary policy, which means having a larger or smaller budget deficit.

Interviewer And this happens in America, in Germany?

Gabriel Mangano Mainly in Germany. The two most independent central banks we can think of are really Switzerland and Germany.

Interviewer Not the Fed, the Federal Reserve?

Gabriel Mangano The Fed, yes, but the Fed is slightly less independent, in the sense that, for instance, it doesn't have a goal of price stability as clearly stated as the German or the Swiss central banks, for instance.

Interviewer But you think the independent bank is a model for the future?

Gabriel Mangano Yes, I would argue it is not, it should not be completely independent. Actually I'm working presently on something that tends to show that the independence should actually be adapted to the economic conditions in the country and outside the country, but yes, generally a more independent central bank is certainly more, well certainly more desirable than a non-independent central bank.

English for Business Studies Second Edition
© Cambridge University Press 2002

5 False (He says that although the goal of price stability is not *as clearly stated* as in Germany or Switzerland, it remains a goal.)

6 True (He says that central bank independence should 'be adapted to the economic conditions in the country and outside the country.')

1d Discussion

In a country with an independent central bank, the government cannot manipulate the money supply, but it can, of course, plan its taxation and spending policies with the date of the next election in mind.

Many politicians in left-of-centre (social democratic) parties believe that governments should have the possibility to reflate a depressed economy, in order to reduce unemployment, according to the tenets of Keynesianism (see Units 25 and 26). This requires the ability to increase the money supply, and leads many Keynesians to argue that the central bank should be controlled by the elected government, rather than by bankers, who are generally unsympathetic to Keynesian ideas and more concerned with preserving price stability than reducing the level of unemployment. The Western European countries which adopted the euro in 2002 lost the ability to manipulate their money supply or interest rates.

2 Taxation

2a Discussion

Benjamin Franklin (1706–90) was an American statesman (he helped write the Declaration of Independence) and a scientist (he invented the lightning conductor). His line about death and taxes is still widely quoted.

> **ANSWERS**
>
> In most countries, consumers pay sales tax or value-added tax on most products sold in department stores.

Most people pay income tax on their wages or salary (unless this is extremely low).

Inheritances are usually subject to a capital transfer tax.

Gains from shares and other securities are often liable to capital gains tax.

Most countries have customs duties on imports, either from all foreign countries, or from those not part of a customs union such as the EU or NAFTA.

Other common taxes include excise duties on petrol, tobacco and alcohol; road tax on cars; and stamp duty on property and financial transactions.

2b Vocabulary

> **ANSWERS**
>
> | | | | | |
> |---|---|---|---|---|
> | **1** B | **2** A | **3** A | **4** B | **5** C |
> | **6** A | **7** B | **8** C | **9** C | **10** B |

2c Reading

> **ANSWERS**
>
> **A** The functions of taxation
> **B** Advantages and disadvantages of different tax systems
> **C** Tax evasion
> **D** Avoiding tax on salaries
> **E** Avoiding tax on profits

Vocabulary notes

– *Loopholes* is of course pronounced loop-holes, not loofoles.

– *Riches* is another word for wealth, but *rich* and *poor* never take an s: we talk about *the rich* and *the poor* (but never *the poors*).

– French speakers sometimes wrongly think that *inherit* (like *inhabited*) is a negative (because of the French verbs *hériter*, *habiter*).

- *Deduct* (to subtract or take away) and *deduce* (to infer by reasoning from facts), do not mean the same thing in English, although in French, Spanish and Italian the same verb has both meanings (as does the English expression *to make a deduction*).

- In several languages, the equivalent term for *tax haven* uses a translation of the word *paradise*, a synonym for *heaven* (e.g. Steuerparadies, paradis fiscal, paradiso fiscale). But *haven* means harbour (*Hafen* in German, *havre* in French).

An additional question

If, in 1986, as mentioned in the text, Britain and Italy were the world's fifth and sixth largest industrial economies, what were the first four?

(*Answer*: The USA, Japan, (West) Germany, France.)

2d Comprehension

ANSWERS

1 True (Excise duties on cigarettes and alcohol are (in theory) designed to discourage spending on these goods, while tax laws allowing accelerated depreciation of capital investments are designed to encourage spending.)

2 True (If you pay tax on dividends, this amount of money is being taxed for the second time. If you spend your dividends, you will probably pay a sales tax or VAT. If you don't spend them, you might pay wealth tax every year on the money.)

3 True (The text describes this as a disincentive to working.)

4 False (Poorer people have to spend a greater *proportion* of their income on consumption.)

5 True

6 False (Loopholes are legal ways of paying less tax; this is called tax *avoidance*.)

7 False (This merely delays taxation. You pay tax when you receive your pension or the sum of the life-insurance policy.)

8 True

2e Vocabulary

ANSWERS

1 depreciation   2 disincentive
3 regressive   4 consumption
5 self-employed   6 national insurance
7 perks   8 tax shelters   9 tax-deductible
10 tax havens

2f Discussion

The **cartoon**, like the ones in Units 2, 17, 19 and 26, once again seems to ridicule business people (although the men portrayed could equally be politicians, economists, or just people with high incomes). Cartoons about managers, economists and bankers almost invariably ridicule them, whether they are found in literary magazines such as the *New Yorker* or on the financial pages of newspapers. Appalling managers, of course, also appear almost daily in Scott Adams' widely syndicated *Dilbert* cartoon strip. (See also http://www.unitedmedia.com/comics/dilbert.) Cartoons about lawyers, accountants and R&D scientists are also generally negative, at least in the USA and Britain. This might be worth discussion. Do these groups of people deserve their reputations? Do they have a similarly bad reputation in other countries? If not, who does?

ANSWERS

Speech bubbles 1, 3, 6, 9, 10, 12 and 15 are clearly in favour of taxation and government spending (on the transport infrastructure, health, welfare, the urban environment, education, etc.). Speech bubbles 2, 4, 5, 7, 8, 11, 13, 14 and 16 are clearly against taxation.

2g Writing

Even learners without opinions of their own should be able to construct a short talk or report from the material in **2f**. Seeing both sides of the argument, and therefore using phrases such as 'on the other hand' and 'nevertheless' should not be too difficult either.

New words in this unit

budget deficit	monetary policy
capital gains tax	moonlighting
capital transfer tax	political business cycle
direct tax	price stability
disincentive	progressive tax
exchange rate	regressive
excise duties	sales taxes
fiscal policy	tax avoidance
government spending	tax evasion
indirect tax	tax haven
inflation	tax loss
inflationary	tax shelters
laundering money (or	taxation
money laundering)	underground
lender of last resort	economy
loophole	wealth tax

Unit 24 | Exchange rates

The value of a country's currency is extremely important to all businesses engaged in international trade – imports and exports. For over a quarter of a century after the second world war, most major currencies were pegged against the US dollar, which in turn was fixed against gold. Since the early 1970s, there has been a system of managed floating exchange rates, largely determined by supply and demand, which in theory reflect a country's balance of payments and rate of inflation. In fact, many currency movements seem to be influenced by speculation rather than underlying economic activity. Currency speculation in Western Europe was greatly reduced by the adoption of a common currency, the euro, by twelve countries in 2002.

This unit contains a text that gives the recent history of exchange rates, and summarizes arguments for and against both floating rates and a common currency, and an interview with an economist who defends the floating rate system and talks about the necessity for a common European currency.

1 From fixed to floating exchange rates

1a Discussion

A possible opening discussion question: How many names of currencies can you think of in 60 seconds? (European currencies abolished by the introduction of the euro should be included, otherwise European learners might find this rather difficult.)

ANSWERS

2 Because of inflation; and because of interest.

3 Because under a system of floating exchange rates, the value of currencies, which depends on supply and demand, is constantly fluctuating on foreign exchange markets. (See paragraph B of the text in **1b**.)

If the learners know the answer to question 3 (floating exchange rates), the history of exchange rates can be discussed before reading the text, by way of questions such as:

- Have there always been floating exchange rates?
- What was decided at Bretton Woods in 1944?
- When did the Bretton Woods system collapse, and why?

(The answers to these questions are to be found in the text in **1b**.)

Vocabulary note It might be worth mentioning the difference between 'worth less' and 'worthless'.

1b Reading

ANSWERS

A The period of gold convertibility

B Floating exchange rates

C The abolition of exchange controls

D Intervention and managed floating exchange rates

E The power of speculators and the collapse of the EMS

F Why many business people would prefer a single currency

G The introduction of the single European currency

1c Comprehension

ANSWERS

1 False (Following inflation, there was not enough gold.)

---

2 False (Anybody can buy gold with dollars, but the Federal Reserve is not obliged to exchange dollar bills for gold.)

3 True (We say that floating currencies appreciate or depreciate.)

4 False (Floating currencies appreciate or depreciate.)

5 True

6 True

7 True

8 False (A currency that depreciated 100% would be worth absolutely nothing.)

1d Vocabulary

ANSWERS

1 1 B   2 D   3 A   4 C   5 F   6 E

2 1 adjust   2 convert   3 abolish
   4 suspend   5 fluctuate   6 diverge

Note In question 3, 'exchange controls used to limit…' contains the verb *used to* relating to the past; this is *not* the same as the passive form of the verb *to use*, as in 'Exchange controls are used to limit…'

1e Discussion

More information about the Tobin Tax is available from its defenders in the US and Britain, on http://www.ceedweb.org/iirp/ and http://www.tobintax.org.uk/.

2 Floating exchange rates versus a common currency

2a Vocabulary

You would *not* normally expect to hear the following expressions in this context:

accelerated depreciation, which is an accounting technique

cash flow, which refers to a business's finances

floating rate note, which refers to bonds and similar securities, not to currencies or banknotes

flotation, which is the act of selling the shares of a company to the public (in the US, also known as an *initial public offering*)

managed fund, which is a pool of investors' money

off-the-peg, which means ready-to-buy, requiring no alteration

One could reasonably expect to find the other expressions in an interview about exchange rates, and indeed all of them appear in the recording.

2b Listening 🔊

TAPESCRIPT

Interviewer Professor Lambelet, I imagine that you are in favour of freely floating exchange rates, in principle …

Prof. Lambelet Oh, that's much too global a question. It depends on circumstances. You know if you had a world currency you'd have no exchange rates, and that presumably would be good for trade, it would mean, you know, like under the gold standard, a very stable and certain economic environment, but then you would also need to have a world central bank, and that's quite a tall order, so, you know, I think we should take a kind of pragmatic approach and say that in a world where economic policies diverge, very often, or where coordination is often an empty word, floating exchange rates are a kind of second best.

Interviewer So, when you say second best, best would be a world currency with a world central bank?

Prof. Lambelet That's debatable, you see, because it would not be enough to have a world central bank, because you'd also need to have some kind of world fiscal system to cushion whatever shocks may happen in parts, only in parts of the world – if it's a global shock everyone suffers alike so there's no problem. A kind of managed floating system is best for Europe. At one point, you know, there will have to be a jump, I mean to a common currency. When that will take place I don't know, I wouldn't expect it to be very soon.

Interviewer But the current managed floating system doesn't seem to work too well. The speculators or the market seems to be much stronger than any government or any central bank intervention.

Prof. Lambelet That's true, and sometimes the markets may overreact. But again, let's be practical. You know, pure floating maybe would be too unstable a system. Pegged exchange rates run into severe problems with capital flows, so a kind of, you know, half and half system whereby central banks do intervene and try to calm things down, where you may have target zones, I think, that's, you know it's muddling through all right, but, you know, that's how we live.

Interviewer But the volatility we've had for the last 10 or 20 years in exchange rates, it wasn't predicted by the people who said that freely floating or floating exchange rates would always be more accurate than a gold standard or a pegged system.

Prof. Lambelet That's certainly true. Er, there had been a precedent incidentally, you know, when Friedman, Milton Friedman made himself an advocate of floating exchange rates, that was back in 1953, there was a precedent, as I said, in the 1920s, there you had a floating…and the experience was bad. I would however say that…there is a learning element in that. Let me take an example. In 78, there was a very strong speculative move on the Swiss franc, and the franc increased a lot, appreciated a lot, something like 25% within three months. I don't think that this is likely to happen again, because markets have I think learned a little at least not to overreact in that way. But it's not a perfect system.

English for Business Studies Second Edition
© Cambridge University Press 2002

ANSWERS

1 True (He says 'presumably'.)
2 True (A 'tall order' means a highly unlikely event.)
3 True (He say that 'coordination is often an empty word'.)
4 False (He says that a world fiscal system would be necessary to cushion shocks that happen only in parts of the world.)
5 True (He says that 'at one point there will have to be a jump'.)
6 False (He says that they also existed in the 1920s.)
7 Tentative answer: False (Because with currencies, 'attack' generally means to sell and cause to depreciate, rather than to buy. Yet causing a currency to rise 25%, with all the consequences for exports and tourism, against the wishes of a government and central bank, *could* also be thought of as an attack.)
8 True

2c Comprehension 🔊

ANSWERS

1 D	2 C	3 B	4 A	5 E
6 G	7 F			

An additional **writing** exercise would be to ask the learners to do some research, if necessary, and write a short history (200 words) of their national currency. (Over the past half-century, has it been fixed, or freely floating, or managed floating?)

New words in this unit

currency	managed (or dirty)
devaluation	floating exchange
exchange controls	rate
fixed exchange rate	overvalued
floating exchange rate	parity
freely (or clean)	pegged
floating exchange	purchasing power
rate	parity
gold convertibility	revaluation
	undervalued

Unit 25 | The business cycle

As everybody knows, market economies regularly experience periods of expansion and of contraction. There seems to be a permanent and unavoidable business cycle of booms and recessions, upturns and downturns. This unit contains both a text and an interview with an economist dealing with the various causes of the business cycle. (The issue of whether the government is able to *do* anything about the business cycle is left until the following unit.)

1 What causes the business cycle?

There is an exercise on **describing graphs** in the Language reference section of the Student's Book.

1a Vocabulary

> **ANSWERS**
>
> 1 depression   2 trough   3 upturn or expansion or recovery   4 peak
> 5 recession or downturn or contraction
> 6 boom

Pronunciation note Learners unfamiliar with the word *trough* will probably not be able to guess its correct pronunciation (/trof/), given that there are at least nine different ways of pronouncing the letters -*ough* in English, as in *though, through, thought, thorough, trough, tough, bough, hiccough* and *lough* (the Irish version of the Scottish *loch* or lake). The 1995 *Concise Oxford English Dictionary* also gives the archaic word *hough* (pronounced 'hock'), which makes ten, but your learners do *not* need to know this!

1b Reading

> **ANSWER**
>
> Reasons mentioned in the text include changes in the level of consumption, resulting from changes in interest rates or changes in people's beliefs about the future, and changes in the level of wages and salaries, all of which lead to changes in the level of investment; and technological, and political and demographic changes.

1c Comprehension

> **ANSWERS**
>
> 1 B   2 I   3 A   4 E   5 F
> 6 G   7 D   8 C   9 H
> (2 C – 'Companies only invest if their company's sales are increasing' – would clearly be grammatically bizarre.)

1d Vocabulary

> **ANSWERS**
>
> 1 expectations   2 mortgage   3 rent
> 4 output   5 investment   6 industrialists
> 7 consumption   8 lay off
> 9 demographic   10 austerity

1e Discussion

Once again, there are no 'right answers', although business students may well have an opinion. Similarly, they can reasonably be expected to know whether the economic situation in the country is good or bad, and whether it is expected to improve or worsen.

2 Economic theory and the business cycle

2a Listening 🔊

> ### TAPESCRIPT
>
> *Kate Barker* The traditional theory of the business cycle is that it's caused by upturns and downturns in the behaviour of companies, in terms of mostly their investments and of their stocks, and in particular the fact that when demand pressure is very strong, that companies are running at very high levels of capacity, they're using their plant to the full, and then they tend to invest perhaps overmuch, and if demand weakens a little bit you have an overreaction in investment, people stop investing completely, that feeds right back into the stock cycle, and pushes the economy down from a high level, down to a low level, and it may stay at the low level until companies have to invest to replace investment, rather than investing to increase capacity. And that was the, that was the standard theory of the cycle.
>
> It was turned on its head, in a sense, in the 1970s and 80s, when we had two cycles in the industrialized world that were not driven by investment at all, but were driven by shortages of particular commodities, and in particular oil, very sharp rise in the oil price in both the early 70s and the early 1980s. But if you look at the last cycle we've just had in Britain and also in Europe, that was back to the old theory of the cycle, it was driven by overinvestment. In the late 1980s, because of two factors, financial deregulation and the expectations of very strong growth as a result of the coming of the single market in the European Community, businessmen in Europe overinvested, and when the shock of German reunification raised interest rates and demand fell away sharply, because capacity was so strong investment also fell away very strongly, and exacerbated the

> following recession, so that we had two or three years of strongly negative growth, and it's really taken us three or four years to recover from that overinvestment cycle.
>
> *English for Business Studies Second Edition*
> © Cambridge University Press 2002

> ### ANSWERS
>
> 1   b
> 2   a
> 3a They increase their productive capacity by too great an extent ('they tend to invest perhaps overmuch').
> 3b They stop *all* investment, modernization and expansion ('you have an overreaction in investment, people stop investing completely').
> 4   When they have to replace out-of-date equipment ('have to invest to replace investment, rather than investing to increase capacity').
> 5   Shortages of particular commodities, particularly oil.
> 6   The deregulation of financial markets, and expectations of growth due to the forthcoming single European market.
> 7   The reunification of East and West Germany, which led to an increase in interest rates (first in Germany, then elsewhere).

2b Listening 🔊

> ### TAPESCRIPT
>
> *Kate Barker* The standard classical theory of the economy, the theory that we all tend to begin with when we learn about economics, suggests that it's very, that economies naturally return to an equilibrium level, where they make full use and efficient use of all their resources. But most of the textbooks, when they're moving to teach

that model, also mention the fact that there are a number of very strong assumptions to make that model work. There has to be perfect competition, there has to be a lack of exogenous shocks, shocks from the world outside in terms of exchange rates or commodity prices to the system, there has to be perfect information, so everybody knows exactly what's going on in the market at any one time, and the responses have to be very quick. Industrialists have to adjust their prices very quickly, wage-setters have to adjust their wages very quickly. In the real world we know that people do not adjust prices and they do not adjust wages so quickly. We know that people make a lot of mistakes in terms of information, they see the future incorrectly, and they're often surprised by developments in the external environment which they haven't seen. And it's these kind of mistakes that lead us into downturns which then become self-fulfilling, because as they go down and people think they're going to go on down further, the economy runs down, runs down itself, and the natural tendency to return to equilibrium that the classical economist would see takes a very, very long time to operate, and it's in that sense that Keynes said 'In the long run, we're all dead.' And his belief was that the government, by changing expectations from the slowing down, or self-fulfilling slowing down into a self-fulfilling moving up, could bring the economy back into equilibrium a little bit faster. Keynes's theory really revolves around making the natural processes that bring the economy back towards equilibrium work rather more quickly, because he believed that if you, if left to themselves, you could stay at a very low level of demand for what would seem like a lifetime.

English for Business Studies Second Edition
© Cambridge University Press 2002

ANSWERS

1 1 equilibrium   2 resources
   3 assumptions   4 perfect competition
   5 exogenous   6 exchange   7 commodity
   8 information   9 industrialists

2 Mistakes regarding future economic developments.

3 If people believe that the economy will go into recession – even if this belief is based on incorrect information – and therefore invest or consume less, they can in this way bring about a recession. When a recession begins, if people reduce their investment and consumption still further, the recession will continue and get worse.

4 Keynes meant that even if economies do have a natural tendency to return to a full-employment equilibrium 'in the long run', this could be an extremely long time, which might seem like a lifetime.

5 He said that the government could change people's expectations, and make them think that the economy would expand again.

Note Precisely how Keynes believed the government could stimulate the economy and bring it back into an equilibrium a little bit faster – by increasing the money supply, or lowering taxes, or increasing government spending, in this way ending people's expectations of a continuing recession – is discussed in the following unit.

New words in this unit

assumptions	exogenous
austerity	expansion
balance of payments	gross domestic
boom	product (GDP)
consumption	industrialists
contraction	peak
demographic	recovery
depression	save
downswing	slump
endogenous	stocks
equilibrium	trough

Unit 26 | Keynesianism and monetarism

The major macroeconomic argument for the past 60 years or so has been whether governments can effectively intervene in the business cycle, and move economies away from recessions more quickly than would otherwise happen. Classical economic theory argued that economies tended towards an equilibrium in which all resources were used. The depression of the 1930s showed that, at least in the short term, this was untrue. John Maynard Keynes argued that by increasing its own spending, or the amount of money in circulation, a government could stimulate demand and boost a contracting economy. For over a quarter of a century after the second world war, the governments in many industrialized countries successfully used Keynesian policies. But after the oil crisis in 1973–4, many countries began to experience 'stagflation' – a prolonged recession or stagnation at the same time as high inflation. For monetarist economists, this showed that although Keynesian attempts to increase demand and reduce unemployment worked in the short term, the only long-term effect was to increase inflation. In recent years, neo-Keynesians have revived the argument for government action. This unit contains both a text and an interview with an economist about Keynesianism, monetarism, unemployment and inflation.

1 The business cycle and government intervention

Pronunciation note *Keynes* sounds like *canes* and not *keens*.

Cartoon: Learners can be asked to work out from the context the meaning of *sluggish* (slow-moving, at a low level of activity) and *buoyant* (at a high level of activity).

1a Discussion

Many economists argue that any government intervention in the business cycle merely worsens the situation. If the government borrows and spends money, this leaves less money available for the private sector to borrow for new investments, and possibly raises interest rates. (Economists call this 'crowding out'.) It also creates a debt that will have to be repaid at some stage. Furthermore, the positive effects of government spending will quite likely occur too late, when the economy is already on an upswing.

Of course, a government *could* require unemployed construction workers or teachers to work, without borrowing money, by only paying them the amount they would otherwise receive in unemployment benefits, but this is unlikely to be popular among the people, trades and professions concerned.

1b Vocabulary

> ### ANSWERS
>
> 1 1 F   2 E   3 D   4 A   5 C
>   6 B
> 2 flexible – variable, error – mistake, companies – firms, costs – expenses, excess – surplus, output – production, expenditure – spending, boost – stimulate, increase – raise, lower – reduce
> 3 contraction – growth, boom – depression, flexible – rigid, buoyant – sluggish, cut – increase, deflate – stimulate, demand – supply, consuming – saving

Vocabulary note *Lower* is both a verb and an adjective; *higher* is only an adjective.

1c Reading

Vocabulary note The nouns *long run*, *short run*, *long term* and *short term* are not usually hyphenated; the adjectives *long-run*, etc. usually are.

1d Comprehension

POSSIBLE ANSWERS

1 If people are pessimistic about the future, and fear that they might lose their jobs, they will spend less and save more. This will result in lower demand and, consequently, lower output, employment and investment.

2 Classical theory argues that if people save a lot of money, interest rates will fall, which will encourage business to borrow money and invest.

3 'Demand management' means attempting to reduce the level of demand during an inflationary boom, and increasing it during a recession.

4 Even a small increase in government spending will lead to a larger increase in output because most of the money will be repeatedly respent by its new owners, apart from the proportion they choose to save.

5 By 'the neutrality of money', monetarists mean that the only effect of increasing the amount of money in circulation is to increase prices, and not demand and output.

6 Classical theory argues that a recession will end as soon as businesses and employees recognize the necessity to reduce prices and wages.

7 Monetarist or neo-classical economists argue that government intervention in the business cycle usually comes too late, and so can easily do more harm than good.

8 Neo-Keynesians argue that prices and wages do not adapt to small market changes because companies do not have sufficient information, because there are costs involved in regularly changing prices, and because contracts and labour legislation make it difficult to reduce wages.

2 Inflation and unemployment

These are typical newspaper **headlines**. The top two refer to interest rates. The third and fourth refer to government projects designed to reduce unemployment. The fifth and eighth announce increases in the rate of unemployment. The sixth announces that inflation is falling in the major industrialized countries. (The OECD is the Organization for Economic Cooperation and Development, whose members include most western European countries, the USA and Canada, Australia and New Zealand, and Japan.) The seventh predicts that the government or central bank will raise interest rates.

2a Listening 🔊

TAPESCRIPT

Kate Barker The traditional, traditional Keynesian theory suggested that if you increased your budget deficit that it would be possible to boost, to boost domestic demand, and that people would spend, spend more money that would feed on into the economy through the multiplier, through the multiplier effect.

 Today Keynesians are much more cautious about that, and they recognize that if you increase your fiscal deficit, because you drive interest rates up and because you make it more difficult for businesses to invest because interest rates are higher, it's actually very much more difficult for the government acting alone to lift the economy out of recession, in a very simple and direct sense. However, most Keynesians would still consider that there is some role for the government, that they are not completely powerless, in terms of what they can do, in terms of fiscal policy.

The basic theory of the monetarists is that any change in policy that raises the money supply will feed immediately into higher prices, and therefore have no permanent effect in increasing demand. Keynesians argue, in contrast to that, that because information flows are very imperfect, that it's quite possible to increase the money supply a little bit, and make people *think* that demand is running more strongly, and invest a little bit more, and therefore lift economies away from the bottom of recessions earlier than they otherwise would have been. The Keynesian theory certainly doesn't argue that it can dispose of the business cycle altogether. What it does argue is that it can make the business cycle a little bit flatter. The monetarist theory tends to argue on the other hand that because policy is a very difficult thing to use and because monetary policy acts in an extremely powerful way, that actually if you use interventionist policy you may actually accentuate cycles, you could actually make them worse.

English for Business Studies Second Edition
© Cambridge University Press 2002

ANSWERS

1 True ('traditional Keynesian theory suggested that if you increased your budget deficit that it would be possible to boost, to boost domestic demand, and that people would spend, spend more money that would feed on into the economy.')

2 False ('domestic' here means in the country as a whole.)

3 True ('if you increase your fiscal deficit, because you drive interest rates up and because you make it more difficult for businesses to invest because interest rates are higher.')

4 True ('The basic theory of the monetarists is that any change in policy that raises the money supply will feed immediately into higher prices, and therefore have no permanent effect in increasing demand.')

5 True ('Keynesians argue, in contrast to that, that because information flows are very imperfect, that it's quite possible to increase the money supply a little bit, and make people *think* that demand is running more strongly, and invest a little bit more.')

6 False ('The Keynesian theory certainly doesn't argue that it can dispose of the business cycle altogether.')

7 False ('The monetarist theory tends to argue on the other hand that because policy is a very difficult thing to use and because monetary policy acts in an extremely powerful way, that actually if you use interventionist policy you may actually accentuate cycles, you could actually make them worse.')

2b Listening 🔊

TAPESCRIPT

Kate Barker Most economists would nowadays agree on two things, that in the short run it may be possible to increase employment at the cost of slightly higher inflation, but they will also feel that in the long run there is actually very little trade-off between inflation and unemployment, and that if you have an increase in employment that is brought about because you have allowed inflation to increase, that the economy will then have to be reined back, typically in the industrialized world nowadays somebody will raise interest rates, in order to get inflation down, and that will then raise unemployment, so that over the longer term there actually *isn't* a conflict between inflation and unemployment, and most of the industrialized world is now run with the aim of keeping inflation relatively low and stable, because the belief is that in the long run, that will tend to mean that unemployment will be also be kept relatively low. There is, however, I think, a little bit of a flaw in this theory, because it's perfectly possible to keep inflation low and stable by perpetually running your economy a little bit below the capacity level that would use up all the resources, and that's absolutely fine if your only goal is inflation, but if you do have concerns about the social costs, then you have to say that you haven't really solved that problem, but you aren't going to solve it by letting inflation increase. The way you are going to solve it is by improving what is known as the supply side of the economy, by raising your level of capacity, or by raising the quality and qualifications of your work force, so that you can simultaneously keep inflation low and allow unemployment to fall.

English for Business Studies Second Edition
© Cambridge University Press 2002

ANSWERS

1 B ('Most economists would nowadays agree on two things, that in the short run it may be possible to increase employment at the cost of slightly higher inflation, but they will also feel that in the long run there is actually very little trade-off between inflation and unemployment.')

2 C ('the economy will then have to be reined back, typically in the industrialized world nowadays somebody will raise interest rates, in order to get inflation down.')

3 B ('most of the industrialized world is now run with the aim of keeping inflation relatively low and stable, because the belief is that in the long run, that will tend to mean that unemployment will be also be kept relatively low.')

4 A ('it's perfectly possible to keep inflation low and stable by perpetually running your economy a little bit below the capacity level that would use up all the resources.')

5 B ('The way you are going to solve it is by improving what is known as the supply side of the economy, by raising your level of capacity, or by raising the quality and qualifications of your work force.')

New words in this unit

boost	full employment
deflationary	Keynesianism
demand	monetarism
disequilibrium	supply
economic agents	

Unit 27 | International trade

Economists are almost unanimously in favour of free trade, according to the principle of absolute or comparative advantage: if all countries produce and exchange the goods and services in which they have the highest relative productivity, resources are put to their best possible use, and everyone is richer as a result. Unfortunately, free trade also causes much economic disruption, as cheaper production, for whatever reason, in one part of the world, leads to the destruction of existing industries and jobs in other parts of the world. Furthermore, many countries have reached advantageous trading positions by protecting their own industries from international competition for a long period of time, while other countries achieve low-cost production by methods that are not politically acceptable in many democracies. There are consequently many social and political reasons that lead politicians and electors to oppose free trade. In recent years there have been huge demonstrations against globalization at international government summit meetings. This unit contains a text about international trade and protectionism, an interview with an economist who talks about the advantages and disadvantages of free trade for different types of countries, and a writing exercise based on a specific trade dispute between the US and Europe.

1 The growth of international trade

1a Discussion

This short discussion activity is a natural introduction to the topic.

Most young people throughout the world possess some cheap clothes or shoes manufactured in Asia. Most of us regularly eat food from other continents (especially fruit and spices). Many of us possess consumer durables imported from other industrial countries (Japan, the USA, Germany, France, Britain,

Italy, and so on). Many products sold throughout Europe are manufactured in one single country (e.g. most CDs seem to be manufactured in Germany).

1b Vocabulary

Some of this vocabulary could probably be elicited from the learners without looking at the book, *before* doing activity **1b**, by way of questions such as:

– What do we call goods that go from one country to another? (Visible exports and imports)

– What about services that go from one country to another? (Invisible exports and imports)

– What do we call the difference between a country's total imports and exports of goods? (The balance of trade)

– What do we call the difference between all the money paid out and received by a country? (The balance of payments)

– These balances can either be positive or negative. What are the words we use to describe these situations? (A surplus and a deficit)

– Does [your country] have a trade surplus or deficit? A payments surplus or deficit?

– Which countries famously have trade surpluses? (Japan, Hong Kong, Taiwan, the Middle-Eastern oil-exporting countries)

– What do we call the situation in which a country has no foreign trade? (Autarky)

– Which European country famously tried that between the 1960s and 1980s? (Albania)

– What is the term used to describe attempts to restrict imports into a country? (Protectionism)

– Why is this usually done? (To favour local industries and jobs)

– How can this be done? (With tariffs, quotas, special norms and regulations, and so on)

– Why do economists generally believe in free trade? (Because of the theory of absolute or comparative advantage)

Vocabulary note In English we usually talk about *imports* and *exports*, and not *importation* and *exportation*, although these nouns exist to describe the *act* of importing and exporting.

1c Reading

1d Comprehension

POSSIBLE QUESTIONS

1 What can give a country an absolute or comparative advantage in goods and services over other producers?

2 Why does the theory of comparative advantage seem inadequate to explain international trade?

3 What is an 'infant industry'?

4 What is the advantage of tariffs for the government?

5 What is the advantage of quotas over tariffs?

2 Free trade and unemployment

2a Listening 🔊

Note Professor Singh is unfortunately suffering from an illness which affects his breathing and speaking. We are consequently especially grateful to him for having accepted our request to talk about this subject.

TAPESCRIPT

Interviewer Professor Singh, economists are almost unanimously in favour of free trade, but these days it seems that a great many people in industrialized countries are opposed to it…

Prof. Singh …this is a strange situation, because in the past it was the developing countries who used to worry about free trade leading to disadvantage for them because they didn't have a developed manufacturing industry, they didn't have firms which could compete with large firms from Western countries, but now many countries like Korea, Malaysia and others feel they can compete with advanced countries on a range of products because they've learned the lessons, they've been able to import technology from the rich countries, they've been able to educate their labour forces, set up an infrastructure, and since their wages are lower, they think they can compete. So now the complaints about unfairness of free trade come from people in the rich countries.

Interviewer And what do *you* think about these complaints?

Prof. Singh I think the answer really lies in whether or not the world is moving or operating at a level of full employment, or it isn't, or it is not. When the world economy's growing fast then…and jobs are being created, then people are able to put up with the disruptions which free trade causes. What free trade means is that you may have trained for a job then someone in Osaka

---

learns to produce cars a bit cheaper, and then you in Detroit immediately lose your jobs. Free trade can be very disruptive. But of course it has the advantage that it leads to more efficiency, more output, but people can't put up with that disruption if they just lose their jobs, but if there are other jobs to go to, then they're usually able to bear the pain of being made unemployed for a while, while they can go and look for another job. So really it depends upon the level of world economic activity whether free trade is good for you or not.

English for Business Studies Second Edition
© Cambridge University Press 2002

POSSIBLE ANSWERS

1 Formerly, the less developed countries were against free trade because they didn't have competitive manufacturing industries.

2 Countries like South Korea and Malaysia are competitive today because they've been able to import technology from the rich countries, educate their labour forces, and set up an infrastructure.

3 Free trade is *disruptive*; in other words it causes big economic changes, such as the closing down of an entire industry in a country, as the product begins to be made more cheaply somewhere else.

4 The advantage of free trade is that it leads to more efficiency and output.

5 People in industrial countries can only put up with the disruption caused by free trade if they can quite quickly find a new job.

2b Listening 🔊

TAPESCRIPT

Interviewer What about the effect of free trade on countries that are less industrialized?

Prof. Singh Well, the point is the fact of free trade is that they may never industrialize because the thing is that they start with an enormous disadvantage. Suppose you want to produce cars in Africa. Well, how are you going to do that, unless they were heavily subsidized, because you can't compete with the existing car producers, so obviously countries which have not industrialized at all, they need a period of protection for their industry in order for them to make it strong enough to compete in international markets.

Interviewer So how are economists or governments in the rich countries going to convince people of the benefits of free trade?

Prof. Singh If you are talking about free trade, then the best way to promote free trade is to ensure that other measures are taken at the international economic level – cooperation between leading countries to ensure that there is more or less full employment in the rich countries.

But what is also clear is that if the unemployment problem – mass unemployment in the rich countries, 10% unemployment in Germany, in France and near 10% in this country – if these problems are not solved then people will walk away from free trade, and the world will be poorer as a result, so in order to sustain free trade, it is essential that governments tackle the unemployment problem. The other point is that no country on its own in an interdependent world economy can deal with the unemployment problem just on its own in a single country, it can only be dealt with by cooperation between countries, that the big countries have to coordinate their economic policies, but there is no prospect, unfortunately, at the moment, that they are willing to do so.

English for Business Studies Second Edition
© Cambridge University Press 2002

1 If African countries wanted to develop a car industry they would need a period of protection during which the industry was heavily subsidized until it was strong enough to compete in international markets.

2 International economic cooperation among the major industrialized countries.

3 People will abandon ('walk away from') free trade, which will lead to the world becoming poorer.

4 No; he sees no prospect of the major countries cooperating to end it.

2c Discussion

The answers here obviously depend on the country. Business students should be able to answer these questions without too much difficulty.

2d Vocabulary

ANSWERS

These answers are not definitive; learners may think of other logical ways of linking the words.

1 Economists recommend *free trade* in the commodities in which countries have either an *absolute* or a *comparative advantage*. This is the opposite of imposing barriers.

2 *Visible trade* is goods, *invisible trade* is services, *counter-trade* is the exchange of goods or services without the use of money. Autarky is the absence of foreign trade.

3 A trade *balance* can either be in *surplus* or in *deficit*; there is no direct relation with dumping.

4 *Banking, insurance* and *tourism* are all services (invisible trade); merchandise means goods (visible trade).

5 *Quotas* and *tariffs* are forms of *protectionism*, the contrary of the theory of comparative advantage.

6 *Norms* and *quotas* are *non-tariff barriers*; taxes are a tariff.

7 *Tariff barriers* are often imposed to protect *infant industries* being developed as a means of *import substitution*. There is no relation here with barter.

8 Many Third World countries have to *reschedule* or *rollover* their foreign *debt*. There is no direct relation here with trade.

9 To *protect*, to *subsidize*, and to find *substitutes* for imports are the contrary of liberalizing trade.

3 Case study: The banana wars

ANSWERS

1 although   2 as   3 Furthermore or Moreover
4 for example   5 Yet   6 due to   7 however
8 whereas   9 Consequently   10 In other
words   11 Furthermore or Moreover
12 Nevertheless.

'However' could be used in (5), but 'Yet' cannot be used in (7), as it has to come at the beginning of a clause.

New words in this unit

absolute advantage	free trade
autarky	import
balance of trade	import substitution
barter or counter-trade	industrialize
	infant industry
comparative advantage	invisible imports and exports
comparative cost principle	non-tariff barrier
deficit	protectionism
developing countries	quota
division of labour	surplus
dumping	tariff
elastic	visible trade (GB) or
export	merchandise trade
factors of production	(US)

Unit 28 | Economics and ecology

In recent years the quest for economic growth has increasingly come up against a concern for the protection of the natural environment. Ecologists are concerned about the consumption of non-renewable resources, the creation of waste, and the pollution of the land, sea and air. This unit begins with a questionnaire enabling the learners to discuss how 'green' or environmentally-conscious they are. There is an interview with an ecologist about the ways in which waste and pollution might be reduced, and about a system that he has developed for measuring the environmental acceptability or 'eco-efficiency' of all manufactured products. There is also a text about a way of regulating and limiting pollution that is widely favoured by economists: the creation of a market in pollution rights.

1 Ecology and the individual consumer

Discussion

As usual with such activities, the learners can discuss the questionnaire in pairs, and then report their answers to different questions to the whole class. The issue of public transport and private cars frequently leads to animated discussion.

Vocabulary note To be 'green' also has other meanings in English, including to be immature, inexperienced and gullible, or to be pale and unhealthy looking (perhaps because of seasickness), but these days the 'ecologically conscious' meaning is probably the most common.

2 Measuring eco-efficiency

2a Vocabulary

> **ANSWERS**
>
> 1 emissions 2 waste 3 disposal
> (to dispose of) 4 environmentalist
> 5 eco-efficiency

Vocabulary note French speakers should be reminded that *disposer de* is translated as *to have at your disposal*; and that *to dispose of* here means to throw something away, to get rid of it.

2b Listening 🔊

> **TAPESCRIPT**
>
> *Interviewer* Marc Keiser, you've developed an eco-efficiency labelling system for all manufactured products, which we can talk about in a minute. But during your research you've read a huge amount about ecology and economics. I was wondering if there's any, if you would say there's any consensus these days as to the best way to reduce pollution and environmental damage. Should it be by legislation, or should there be some kind of financial incentives for companies to clean up, clean up their processes, or will it just be consumer pressure – that if enough green consumers pressurize a company they will change their methods?
>
> *Marc Keiser* Actually there is not one solution that can be adopted. You must see that there are usually at least three pressure groups that are of importance to make things move. The

first pressure group is the one which includes the consumers, and the consumers' associations. The second one normally concerns the governmental authorities – national and international organizations. And the third one comes from the industry. Now, if you only have – this is the general rule – if you only have one pressure group at a time trying to make things move, normally you won't have any result. For instance in the United States you have a poll carried out by the *New York Times*, which said that about 80% of the people, of the Americans, considered themselves as environmentalists, who are concerned about ecology. Now we know that the United States, the country itself, is consuming an incredible amount of material resources, energy and so on, and also generating lots of waste. This means that one pressure group alone cannot realize real improvements, because on the other side, you have the government which is committed to this issue, but is not currently ready to take strong actions on that, and then you have industry who is normally concerned about quarterly results, and this is a kind of, this hinders any improvement.

English for Business Studies Second Edition
© Cambridge University Press 2002

ANSWERS

1 legislation; financial incentives; consumer pressure.
2 consumers' associations; government; industry.
3 Not on their own. You need at least two groups. Keiser says 'one pressure group alone cannot realize real improvements', and 'this is the general rule – if you only have one pressure group at a time trying to make things move, normally you won't have any result.'
4 consumption of material resources; consumption of energy; generation of waste.

2c Vocabulary 🔊

ANSWERS

| 1 consensus | 2 incentive | 3 poll |
| 4 quarterly results | | |

2d Listening 🔊

TAPESCRIPT

Interviewer Perhaps you could tell us a bit about your eco-efficiency label. I mean, this could be a source of government legislation, or a tool that could be used by companies, producers, themselves. What exactly is this?

Marc Keiser OK, I would say that the methodology I've developed could be used by both. I've seen in my research that companies accept to make some environmental improvements, to improve their performance, ecological performance, but they would like to have a free hand on how to do this improvement. I've…based on that, I've developed a methodology which gives a government a framework, a legal framework, but still leaves a free hand to companies on how to be in accordance with this framework.

The methodology includes three models, three different models, and which are based on the same measuring units, and the same basic elements. These elements are all of quantitative nature. They concern three categories which are material resources, energy, and emissions.

The third model which ought to inform consumers about the environmental acceptability of a product, or eco-efficiency of a product, that's the same, as I define it, should analyse a finite product, for the consumer, from cradle to grave, that is, from the starting manufacturing step to disposal, including consumption and steps in between.

Interviewer And this would be expressed as a number, a coefficient between zero and a hundred?

Marc Keiser That's correct. It would be expressed in so-called 'eco-points', you can name it however you want, but let's say eco-points, on a scale, on a definite scale, ranging from zero up to one hundred, zero being the worst, one hundred being the best.

Interviewer And the consumer in the store can pick and choose?

Marc Keiser That would be the ultimate target. The consumer comes in, looks at the products, sees the label on it, sees that for instance for one product A, the label is giving a number of 50, let's say, and the other, similar product B, has a label number of 60, this would be information for him that product B would be more eco-efficient than product A.

Interviewer But it's only efficient companies which are likely to want to adopt this, unless the government imposes this legislation.

Marc Keiser Yes. The presence of the government is necessary for that. That's why I first talked about the framework which would give free hand for each company to improve whatever they want, as long as, for instance, the final number, the indicator, is increased, or satisfies a certain level. That means no regulatory instrument, no technological definition.

Interviewer But the information is available to all consumers on all products?

Marc Keiser That's right.

English for Business Studies Second Edition
© Cambridge University Press 2002

ANSWERS

1 B ('companies accept to make some environmental improvements, to improve their performance, ecological performance, but they would like to have a free hand on how to do this improvement.')

2 B ('should analyse a finite product, for the consumer, from cradle to grave, that is, from the starting manufacturing step to disposal, including consumption and steps in between.')

3 D ('as long as, for instance, the final number, the indicator, is increased, or satisfies a certain level.')

2e Vocabulary 🔊

ANSWERS

1 a free hand   2 a (legal) framework
3 quantitative   4 from cradle to grave
5 a scale   6 the ultimate target

2f Discussion

The answer to the third question is almost certainly 'Yes'. It would certainly be expensive, and require a lot of work. The answer to number four is uncertain. The learners themselves have partially answered this already in the second and third questions of the questionnaire in **1a**: 'Are you prepared to pay a higher price for products that you know are *not* dangerous for the environment?'; 'Have you ever stopped using a product because you learnt that it was damaging for the environment?'

3 Pollution and market solutions

3a Vocabulary

ANSWERS

1 economical   2 uneconomical   3 economy
4 economics   5 economists   6 economize
7 economic

It will very likely be necessary to stress (or teach) the different meanings of the adjectives *economic* – the basic adjective from economics – and *economical*, meaning cheap, or using a minimum of resources.

3b Reading

The article is from the *Financial Times*, 6 May 1996.

Students may not recognize the word *curbed* in the title, which means cut or reduced.

Pronunciation note The noun *'permit* in the title of this article is stressed on the first syllable; the verb *per'mit* is stressed on the second, as mentioned in Word stress, section 6, in the Language reference section.

> ### ANSWER
>
> The aim of traded pollution permits is to reduce emissions of polluting substances more cheaply than through traditional regulation.

3c Comprehension

> ### ANSWERS
>
> 1 Because they cause global warming.
> 2 He means that all efforts to protect the environment must take account of the necessity of industrial activity, so that the measures taken should be the ones that are the least damaging and expensive for industry.
> 3 It gives companies a financial incentive to reduce emissions, and it greatly reduces the costs and the bureaucracy involved in enforcing environmental legislation.
> 4 They say that the number of permits given to companies is too large – they could easily have cut more emissions.
> 5 Because the system could lead to areas of concentrated pollution if all the companies in a certain region bought pollution permits rather than cutting SO_2 emissions.
> 6 Taxing companies that release carbon into the atmosphere.

3d Vocabulary

> ### ANSWERS
>
> 1 architects 2 advocating 3 pragmatism
> 4 auctioned 5 a fine 6 compliance
> 7 bureaucracy 8 scheme 9 ceiling
> 10 lax 11 tackling 12 toyed with

3e Writing

> ### A POSSIBLE ANSWER
>
> Companies are **allocated** a progressively reduced number of SO_2 **permits** each year. If they want to **emit** more than this amount they can **purchase** permits from other companies. If they are able to **reduce** the amount of SO_2 they produce, they can **sell** their **surplus** permits.

3f Discussion

Some of the disadvantages of the system are mentioned in the article (e.g. the possibility of local concentrated pockets of pollution), while the most common alternative methods of limiting pollution are mentioned in the listening section above.

New words in this unit

cost-effective	environmentalist
eco-efficiency	global warming
ecology	polluter
emission	recycling
energy	waste
environment	

Unit 29 | Information technology and electronic commerce

Information technology continues to make rapid advances – to the extent that it now seems astonishing that the First Edition of this book did not contain a unit on the subject! Most business schools now contain an IT or an e-commerce or an information systems department. Many business students use computers and mobile phones on a daily basis, and may have grown up playing computer games since a young age. Most people remain resolutely upbeat about the utility and potential of computing and the 'new economy', so for a change, this unit contains an article by a professor of information systems which concentrates on the potential dangers of information technology.

There is also an interview with a cinema manager who talks about his cinema's use of the internet and e-mail to keep their customers informed of what's on and to allow them to book tickets, and a role play concerning a shop that sells handheld computers and how it should react to the suggestion that it becomes an internet retailer.

1 The dangers of information technology

1b Reading

The text is slightly adapted from an article in *New Scientist*, 4 March 2000.

After doing discussion activity **1a**, you could ask the learners to anticipate the author's argument: what do you think the article will be about (or as we say, what do you think the article says?) – what are the bad aspects of information technology?

POSSIBLE HEADINGS

1 A new age of communication and the optimists
2 The internet and tax avoidance
3 Globalization and regulation
4 Rich and poor countries and the internet
5 Unrest, crime and terrorism
6 The survival of the fittest

1c Comprehension

ANSWERS

1 Yes ('We are at the threshold of a new age of communication.')
2 Yes ('People are increasingly buying goods and services via the internet from places where sales taxes are lowest.')
3 Yes ('… corporations carry out their transactions in low-tax jurisdictions.')
4 No ('Drugs, crime and terrorism, once localized problems, are now organized globally.')
5 Yes ('Everything is changing, and anyone who does not embrace the change will go under.')
6 No ('Governments will find it more and more difficult to keep track of the activities of corporations.')
7 Yes ('… governments will find it harder to raise taxes … the tax deficit will grow.')
8 No ('… this is likely to remain a "theoretical" possibility.')
9 No ('… the new information technology will disenfranchise large sections of society.')
10 Yes ('Unemployment among the semi-skilled will increase as more production jobs are automated' – though it is possible that information technology will create more skilled jobs than the semi-skilled jobs it replaces.)

11 Yes ('Information warfare will be commonplace between individuals, pressure groups, companies and the state. The dispossessed will hit the capitalists where they are the most vulnerable: in their computer and telecommunications infrastructure.')

12 Yes ('… the new information technology will disenfranchise large sections of society.')

13 No ('The power of the nation state will weaken.')

14 Yes (See the whole of the last paragraph.)

15 No ('For them, the internet is the ultimate democracy. Are they right? I doubt it.')

16 Yes ('Criminals will be able to exploit people in the same way.')

17 No ('… they predict, making life easier for everyone … Are they right? I doubt it.')

18 No ('… rich countries will be among the first to benefit. It won't be so rosy if you're poor.')

1d Vocabulary

ANSWERS

1 A   2 F   3 E   4 D   5 C   6 B

1e Vocabulary

ANSWERS

1 1 the dispossessed   2 disenfranchise
3 evaporating   4 embrace   5 go under   6 rosy
7 off the beaten track   8 be cast into obscurity
9 blind to   10 degenerate (verb)   11 mutate
12 thrive

2 1 evaporating   2 the dispossessed   3 be cast
into obscurity   4 mutate   5 go under
6 embrace   7 disenfranchise   8 off the beaten
track

2 E-commerce

Listening

TAPESCRIPT

Chris Peters My name is Chris Peters and I am the general manager of the Arts Picture House, Cambridge. My responsibilities are for more or less absolutely everything to do with the building, from the operation on the floor downstairs, to running the bar, marketing, publicity, promotions and of course putting together our very diverse and attractive programme of films that we have on offer here.

The internet, the website and the e-mail systems that we use have been sort of foremost in development of the Picture House brand. City Screen, the company behind Picture House, have been pushing that from day one.

…there is a variety of things that you can do. We use it as a marketing tool to plug up-and-coming special events or to tell people about special deals that we have: basic information, like ticket prices, location. But one of the main things is that people can obviously look at our programme, get a review on the programme and obviously of the times that that is showing and then book online, you know, anything up to sort of midday of the day that particular film is showing.

We offer a, you know, we offer a membership scheme here which is very successful. We've got over 4,000 members in total which is streets ahead of any other Picture House cinema, I think the next highest is something like 1,800 to 2,000 so it's, it's a noticeable increase, and what happens, every Monday when the film times are confirmed for the following week, Friday to Thursday, we will e-mail each of our members the film time and the programmes. Again details of any special offers or special events that is happening, every week. So I mean that's a phenomenal task, it takes ages to watch them all go through, but it's, you know it's a worthwhile tool because obviously it's hitting them directly at work or directly at home. Saying *boof*, this is what we've got showing next week, you know; e-mail back or go and visit the website and book now. 'Cause as soon as that goes out we update the box office system and we update the website so they should be able to, the mechanic is that they get the e-mail, they see the film they want to see, they click into the website, book straight away and then their booking's in the bank so to speak.

English for Business Studies Second Edition
© Cambridge University Press 2002

ANSWERS

1 *Possible answer:* The Arts Picture House has a website giving details of its programmes and special offers. It also has a membership scheme and it sends all its members a weekly e-mail with details of the programme. People can book tickets online, either by e-mail or on the internet site.

2 1 running   2 putting together   3 pushing
   4 plug   5 book online   6 hitting

3 1 a long way ahead (i.e. a considerably higher number)
   2 a job requiring a lot of time and effort
   3 it takes a very long time
   4 it's a means or method of marketing that gives positive results (despite all the time and effort it requires)

3 Role play

These are the roles to be photocopied and given to the groups of learners.

ROLE 1

The Store Manager: The Palmtop Shop

You started this business because you thought PDAs and similar gadgets had a great future when you noticed your teenage children and their friends using them. You previously worked in a large television and hi-fi store. You have taken a big risk, setting up your own business, and have borrowed a lot of money to do so, as well as using up all your savings. You think that a website service might bring you in some extra business, but you don't want to spend too much money on it. If e-commerce really takes off in the future, you want to be prepared. Yet you need the advice of people who know more about e-commerce than you do.

English for Business Studies Second Edition
© Cambridge University Press 2002

ROLE 2

The Internet Expert

You are studying business communication systems at university, and working at the Palmtop Shop on Saturdays. You are convinced that e-commerce is the future, especially for products such as PDAs. After all, the world's second-largest PC manufacturer only sells online. Every week you have customers who come in, look at and try out the products, ask you technical questions, and then leave without buying anything, because they can buy PDAs more cheaply on the internet. You think the business should set up a website at once, and eventually close the shop: an e-commerce operation could be run from a much cheaper location than a shop in the high street. It could also have a much lower inventory. You think that if your employer doesn't listen to you and take your advice, his/her business will go bankrupt within a couple of years.

English for Business Studies Second Edition
© Cambridge University Press 2002

ROLE 3

The Salesperson

You have known the manager for years having previously worked together in the TV and hi-fi shop. You are annoyed that he/she is even listening to this inexperienced student with crazy ideas. You believe – in fact you *know* – that customers like to see and touch goods before they buy them. If the shop sets up a website with lower prices it will merely cannibalize its own customers. They will try out the goods in the store and then go home and order them on the net, leaving the shop with no financial advantages whatsoever. Furthermore, you *enjoy* selling and helping customers, which is why you do this job. You do not want to sit in a dull office or warehouse, processing electronic orders.

English for Business Studies Second Edition
© Cambridge University Press 2002

This role play does not require much preparation, and will probably not take very much time. Students may not be able to think up much to say beyond what is written in their role descriptions. There is clearly no 'right answer' as to what the Palmtop Shop should do; a persuasive speaker in any of the four roles may be able to win over the others to his or her views. It is, of course, up to the Store Manager to decide whether he or she makes any decisions. After the role play, the whole class can be invited to give their opinions on both the situation and the discussion they have heard.

ROLE 4

The Sales Representative

You work for a leading manufacturer of PDAs, and have regularly visited the Palmtop Shop since it opened. You are friendly with the owner, having done business with him/her in your previous job, when you represented a hi-fi manufacturer. You only live two minutes away, and you also know the other two members of staff, and have socialized with them on Saturday evenings. You think this particular business is much too small. It is successful, and should increase its activities and also sell other products: mobile phones, laptop computers, and so on. If it expanded, you'd like to work for it, as you are tired of all the travelling involved in your current job. You are undecided about whether the business should ignore e-commerce, add an e-commerce operation, or become only an e-commerce business, but you are convinced that they should expand into new products.

English for Business Studies Second Edition
© Cambridge University Press 2002

New words in this unit

I suspect that there *are* no new technical words in this unit: who doesn't know the words e-mail, internet, information technology, etc.?

Unit 30 | Entrepreneurs and venture capital

The success of a country's economy depends to a large extent on the continuous creation of new companies. This requires both entrepreneurial people and political, legal, educational and financial systems that enable them to start new businesses. As discussed in Unit 22, the government has a role to play here, but so does the private sector, especially regarding the availability of venture capital for new enterprises.

Some countries are more successful than others in creating new companies. There are countries with perfectly good business and engineering schools that produce graduates who are unable to find jobs for which they are qualified. (This may be something you can discuss with your students.)

This unit contains an interview with a financier working for a company that raises finance for new businesses in Britain, and a text about entrepreneurship (indeed, in praise of entrepreneurs), which is critical of the way the 'standard classical theory' of economics, and the general equilibrium model, disregard the role of individual entrepreneurs.

1 Market opportunities and venture capital

1a Discussion

Some business students, and indeed economics students, may nurse dreams of becoming entrepreneurs. Others may accept that it would be unrealistic of them to imagine that they could run their own company. Still others may surprise you by announcing that they are already entrepreneurs, running their own company as well as studying. But perhaps you should have found this out before reaching Unit 30!

1b Vocabulary

ANSWERS
1 B   2 C   3 A   4 B   5 A   6 B   7 B   8 B   9 B

1c Listening 🔊

TAPESCRIPT

Ed Coombes My name is Ed Coombes and I am a corporate finance executive and I work for Cambridge Capital Partners, a small corporate finance team that is regulated by the SFA, and we focus on raising funds for private companies.

  We specialize in the technology, media and telecoms companies. Primarily because ten years ago if you wanted to start one of those companies you needed a lot of money and it took a long time to grow it, then gradually society is demanding products, and so is industry, which are faster to develop and the money necessary to develop them is less, and so, and also the speed to market is less.

  A market opportunity has opened up in the technology, media and telecom sector, compared to ten, fifteen years ago. It's speed of getting a company up and running, money available for it from high net worth individuals, and pension funds who traditionally in the past were risk averse and also like to just invest in the large companies. They are not getting the return on their investment so they recognize they need to take a higher risk, so a smaller potential high growth company, and they get a higher return. That's effectively the market opportunity that has opened up which wasn't around so much ten years ago and in the financial sector, the banking sector, if we take corporate finance services they have recognized this, whereas ten years ago they would only service clients that were listed on exchanges, gradually the corporate finance teams have seen, ah, we need to go and find those companies that are going to list and the next stage was, ah, well before they list they're private companies, and we need to go and help them before they even get to that stage for listing, and so bankers like myself have left the City and are now, we're increasing in number and are seeing there is a market need for corporate finance at the smaller end of the scale. Now for us it's cost effective because when we raise some money, if you're a large bank or a small bank you take your fee in cash. What we do is, we, if we raise, if we're dealing with a small company we can't always take it in cash but we'll take it in equity, which is shares in the company, and the hope is that we take enough cash to cover our running costs and if we take the rest of the fee in equity, shares in the company, then we hope that in two or three years' time this will be a high growth company and ideally it lists on the markets and we can sell our shares then.

English for Business Studies Second Edition
© Cambridge University Press 2002

ANSWERS

1 Investing in technology, media and telecoms companies that develop new products and bring them to market much more quickly than companies used to do.

2 They considered that they were not getting a sufficient return on their traditional investments in large, listed companies, so they began to take the risk of investing in smaller companies with the potential for high growth and a high return.

3 They are partly paid in money (not literally 'in cash'), because they need to cover their running costs, and partly in equity, i.e. shares in the company that they will be able to sell two or more years later if the company is listed on the stock exchange.

Note Ed Coombes mentions the SFA, which is the Securities and Futures Authority, which regulates these sectors of the financial industry in Britain.

1d Listening 🔊

TAPESCRIPT

Ed Coombes Business plans tend to be between 30 and 60 pages long, and so prior to any meeting with the company I like to see what they've written down on paper about themselves. You first of all find a two-page, what we call executive summary, and that is basically an overview of the next 50 pages of what this business plan is roughly about and what you are going to expect to read. The next, the first chapter tends to be what the company is going to do. The second chapter tends to be the market opportunity. The third chapter tends to be the strategy of how they're going to deploy the investment and seize this market opportunity. Fourth chap, fourth chapter tends to be the revenue. Fifth chapter is the competition. Sixth chapter is the management. Seventh chapter is marketing, advertising and normally at the, at the end is the finance needed. There you are, there's a quick business plan for you.

English for Business Studies Second Edition
© Cambridge University Press 2002

ANSWERS

Chapter 2: market opportunity   Chapter 4: revenue   Chapter 5: competition   Chapter 6: management   Chapter 7: marketing and advertising   Chapter 8: finance needed

1e Listening 🔊

TAPESCRIPT

Ed Coombes First of all investors are obsessed with two key things: competition and the revenues. With the competition, they want to know who is there at the moment? How are they going to react when this company comes into the market? Or if there is no one there, who is going to come there as well? Now this sends a signal out to the investor about whether the management really understand the market they're in, and how they're going to react in the future and the fact that they are a little bit focused on the future as well. So they can put in barriers to entry or what we call defend themselves.

The other thing is, with revenues investors don't mind if a company, if it's a start-up, in the first two or three years is making a loss, because they are using the capital invested in them to achieve as great a market penetration as possible … So the investor in that business plan when they are reading it is wanting to see when is the first revenue going to come in. How big is it going to be?

Apart from those two chapters, there are chap, management are key. You tend to want to find people with past experience of their sector, you want to find out if there's any non-executive directors on board. They are very, very critical to young growth companies, but also to mature companies, because the world changes and everybody suffers from myopia, i.e. they can just see their own little spot. They need to be challenged because markets change, customers change, the company needs to change to address its market.

Entrepreneurs tend to be very emotional, very focused, a lot of qualities which are paramount for starting a company, drive, etc., but they can get in the way of investors at a later stage in terms of the style of running the company, the attitude, the relationships between the new shareholder or potential investor/shareholder and the existing management.

English for Business Studies Second Edition
© Cambridge University Press 2002

ANSWERS

1 The parts about competition in the market the company is interested in, and the company's future revenues.
2 They need to know which companies are already on the market, and how they will react to the new entrant, or which other companies are likely to enter the new market.
3 They need to know when the company will receive its first revenue, and how much it will be.
4 They prefer managers with previous experience of the same sector.
5 They are more able to see changes in markets and customers than the full-time managers, who often can't see beyond their own narrow interests.
6 He says that entrepreneurs can be very emotional about their company, and that their style of running the company, and their attitude, can be a problem for potential investors and shareholders.

2 Equilibrium and entrepreneurship

2a Vocabulary

ANSWERS

1 1C 2F 3G 4H 5A 6B 7E 8D
2 a way – a means
   adjustments – small changes
   ceased – stopped or ended
   fully – completely
   opportunity – possibility
   short-lived – temporary
   struggle – fight
   to assume – to suppose or believe
   to occur – to take place
   unimaginable – inconceivable

Vocabulary note *Means* is a singular noun with an *s*.

2b Reading

The 'standard classical theory' of economics, with its equilibrium model, was mentioned by Kate Barker in Unit 25, exercise **2b**. Supply, demand and equilibrium are also defined in Unit 26, exercise **1b**. Barker talks about the unrealistic assumptions that are necessary to make the equilibrium model work; this text is more critical, unfavourably comparing the general equilibrium model with the 'Austrian School's' account of the market as a process which grants an active, subjective role to consumers and entrepreneurs. As mentioned in the teacher's notes to exercise **2d** in Unit 18, this school of economics is perhaps better known for its views on the role of the state – which it believes should be minimal – than for its critique of 'orthodox' neoclassical (or general equilibrium) theory. The ideas in the text are synthesized from various works by Austrian (or Austro-American) economists, including Ludwig von Mises, Friedrich Hayek, Frank Knight, Israel Kirzner, and Ludwig Lachmann.

ANSWERS

A Economic equilibrium
B The problem of change
C The existence of disequilibrium
D Ignorance and alertness
E Perceiving opportunities
F Entrepreneurs and managers

2c Comprehension

ANSWERS

1 True ('Prices and quantities "adjust themselves" in such a way that supply meets demand.')
2 True ('Prices and quantities "adjust themselves" in such a way that supply meets demand.' This includes the price of labour.)
3 False (Even if supply meets demand, badly run businesses might not be able to supply at the right price.)
4 True ('Instead of understanding competition as a process in which participants in a market struggle to beat each other, it describes a state of affairs in which any such struggle is both unnecessary and inconceivable.')
5 False (This is the fundamental criticism of this economic model, which cannot explain long-term recessions, unemployment, etc.)
6 False (It assumes the existence of 'radical ignorance', unawareness of possibilities (as opposed to 'rational ignorance', being ignorant by choice), but it also credits economic agents with 'never-ending change, inquisitiveness, alertness, and creativity.')
7 True ('The entrepreneur discovers a profitable way of satisfying needs. He or she perceives an opportunity to serve the market better than it is currently being served.')
8 True ('Entrepreneurial knowledge consists of the awareness that it is profitable to produce a product, rather than knowledge of *how* to produce it. Like management, technical knowledge is part of the labour input.' Though of course awareness that it is profitable to produce a product is of no use unless the entrepreneur can find people to finance and run a business that actually produces it.)
9 True ('...according to this logic, profit does not come from land, labour, capital, or the technological knowledge of how to turn inputs into outputs, but from mental alertness.')
10 False (To say that 'Many of the best-known entrepreneurs are more interested in – and better at – starting companies than running them. They hire experienced people to do this and move on to a new idea,' is *not* the same as saying that *entrepreneurs in general* are not very good at managing companies – but some of your learners might argue with this answer.)

2d Discussion

Economics students (as opposed to business students) might vociferously defend economic theory, and argue that general equilibrium is just a model, and that to criticize its unreality is misguided.

New words in this unit

business plan	risk averse
entrepreneurship	risky
expectations	running costs
general equilibrium	start-up
non-executive directors	utility

Test 4 | Economics

Note: **This test covers the second half of Unit 18, about competition, as well as Units 20–30.**

Part One: Vocabulary

Which terms are defined below?

1 a group of producers or sellers who combine to avoid competition and increase profits by fixing prices and quantities

2 a loan, usually to buy property which serves as a security for the loan

3 a monopoly in a market or field in which it would not be practical to have competition

4 a panic in which depositors all try to withdraw their money from a bank

5 a period when demand is rising, and an economy is working close to capacity

6 a regular sum of money paid to a retired worker in return for past services or contributions

7 a tax charged on imports

8 anything released into the environment during an industrial process

9 factors which prevent or deter new producers from entering an industry

10 new industries that are not yet large enough to achieve economies of scale and strong enough to compete internationally

11 reductions in unit costs arising from large-scale production

12 the amount of output produced (in a certain period, using a certain amount of inputs)

13 the attempt to reduce imports by producing goods in one's own country

14 the difference between the money values of a country's visible imports and exports

15 the difference between what a country pays for all its imports and receives for all its exports

16 the ending or relaxing of legal regulations or restrictions in a particular industry

17 the exchange of one good for another, without the use of money

18 the system in which a currency could be exchanged for a fixed amount of gold

19 total self-sufficiency and the consequent absence of foreign trade

20 trying to persuade politicians to pass laws favourable to your particular industry

English for Business Studies Second Edition
© Cambridge University Press 2002

Part Two: Comprehension

Are the following statements TRUE or FALSE?

1 Patents give producers a legal monopoly.

2 Companies have a legal obligation to maximize the return on investment they pay their shareholders.

3 Income tax is a form of direct taxation.

4 Tax evasion is legal; tax avoidance is illegal.

5 Accelerated depreciation is a way of encouraging capital investment.

6 Central banks generally fix a country's minimum interest rate.

7 Managed floating exchange rates are determined purely by market forces.

8 Under the Bretton Woods system, the dollar was convertible into gold at a fixed price.

9 An economy contracts after reaching a trough.

10 The theory that money is neutral means that changes in the money supply cannot change prices.

11 Keynesian policy is designed to reduce unemployment.

12 According to the GATT agreement, countries could not grant special trading arrangements to a most favoured nation.

13 The general equilibrium model assumes that, in the long run, supply will always match demand.

14 Entrepreneurs notice profit opportunities – ways of using resources more efficiently.

English for Business Studies Second Edition
© Cambridge University Press 2002

Part Three: Speaking

Allocate each learner one of the following subjects, to speak about for *two minutes*, after ten minutes of preparation with the Student's Book and their course notes.

1 What is the economic theory of perfect competition?

2 What are the economic forces that are diminishing job security?

3 What is the 'stakeholder theory' of corporate responsibility?

4 What, in your opinion, are the most important functions of government?

5 What are the arguments in favour of central bank independence?

6 Why do exchange rates fluctuate?

7 What causes the business cycle?

8 What is the objective of Keynesianism?

9 What are the chief arguments of monetarism?

10 Why are economists generally in favour of international trade?

Part Four: Composition

Possible composition titles:

1 Will the many jobs lost through automation, computing, and 're-engineering' ever be replaced?

2 Do you believe that businesses have social responsibilities beyond increasing their return on equity, and if so, what are they?

3 What, in your opinion, should be the role of government in relation to business and industry? Should there be more or less governmental intervention in the economy in your country?

4 Should the state take an active role in encouraging and developing new technologies, or leave this to the market?

5 What are the functions of a central bank? What are the arguments for making central banks independent from the government?

6 Should, or could, anything be done about the amount of international currency speculation that goes on these days?

7 Is the current system of managed floating exchange rates satisfactory?

8 Market economies inevitably experience slumps as well as booms. What should be the government's response to falls in economic activity?

9 Should there be limits to international trade?

10 It is often suggested that there are three main approaches to reducing pollution – consumer pressure, government legislation, and financial incentives. Which of these appeals to you most, and why?

11 Do you consider current legislation in your country concerning pollution and the environment to be adequate?

12 Which of the following do you think is the most important for an economy – the existence of entrepreneurs, a good supply of capital, a supply of qualified labour, technological innovation, or efficient competition?

ANSWERS

Part One: Vocabulary

1 cartel   2 mortgage   3 natural monopoly   4 bank run   5 boom
6 pension   7 tariff   8 emissions   9 barriers to entry   10 infant industries
11 economies of scale   12 productivity   13 import substitution   14 balance of trade
15 balance of payments   16 deregulation   17 barter   18 gold standard   19 autarky
20 lobbying

Part Two: Comprehension

1 True   2 False   3 True   4 False   5 True   6 True   7 False   8 True
9 False   10 False   11 True   12 True   13 True   14 True

Language reference – Answers

Exercise 1

1 three million, nine hundred (and) eight thousand euros

2 minus one million, three hundred (and) seventy-seven thousand euros

3 thirty million, three hundred (and) seventy-six thousand euros

Exercise 2

1 In my first job, in nineteen seventy-six, I earned thirty-eight pounds a week, which was exactly one thousand nine hundred and seventy-six pounds a year.

2 Today they're buying yen at a hundred (and) nineteen point nine two and selling them at a hundred (and) twenty point oh one.

3 It's either nought point four three one or four point oh three one, I can't remember.

4 A million dollars? But that's over one million ninety thousand euros!

5 No, it's twelve thousand two hundred (and) thirty-one not twelve point two three one!

6 You can fax them on oh double six, double two, two seven, four seven.

7 For further information, call oh one seven one, three five nine, oh one three one.

8 He's two metres eleven tall, like a basketball player.

9 It only cost thirteen euros ninety-five.

10 It's somewhere between two and two-thirds and two and three-quarters.

11 Twenty-seven times three hundred (and) sixty-five is nine thousand eight hundred (and) fifty-five, plus seven for leap years, plus two times thirty-one, and two times thirty, plus sixteen days – I'm ten thousand days old today!

12 The equation is x squared minus y cubed equals z (/zed/ in Britain, /ziː/ in America).

Exercise 3 🔊

This might be the first dictation your learners have done since they left school! The series of 12 utterances is on the recording. After the learners have listened twice, perhaps a volunteer can copy what he or she has written on the blackboard, while reading out the numbers. The class can be asked to correct any mistakes.

1 Why don't you fax her? The number is 001 212 487 1123.

2 His first CD sold 90,010 copies.

3 But the second one has only sold 19,110 so far.

4 The bond was issued at $7\frac{3}{8}$%.

5 The dollar lost 0.0072 against the euro yesterday.

6 I think the three-month inter-bank sterling rate is $5\frac{11}{16}$%.

7 Can you ask him to phone me back next week, on 0161-745 9916?

8 To eight decimal places, pi is 3.14159265.

9 Did you say $(x - y)/z$?

10 No, I said x − y/z.

11 Have you got a calculator? I need to work out the square root of 196.

12 The ISBN, printed on the imprints page, is 0 521 75285X.

Exercise 4

'Annual 'General '**Meet**ing
'British '**Broad**casting Corpo'ration
Chief Ex'ecutive '**Of**ficer
'Cable 'Network **News**
Euro'pean '**Un**ion
'Federal 'Bureau of Investi'**ga**tion
Gross Do'mestic '**Pro**duct
Inter'national '**Bus**iness Ma'chines
Inter'national '**Mon**etary Fund
'Master of '**Bus**iness Adminis'tration
Organi'zation for Eco'nomic Coope'ration and De'**vel**opment
'Doctor of Phi'**los**ophy (abbreviation pronounced *pee aitch dee*)
Re'search and De'**vel**opment
'Total '**Qual**ity 'Management
U'nited '**Na**tions
U'nited States of A'**mer**ica
U'nique '**Sell**ing Propo'sition
'Value 'Added **Tax**
'Very Im'portant '**Per**son
Vice-'**Pres**ident

These names or phrases would also have a main stress, marked in **bold** above.

Exercise 5 🔊

I think manu'facturing will change, con'vert it'self. There are 'many new 'products that have to be in'vented to serve new needs, and they *can* be made in the ad'vanced 'countries be'cause in fact the tech'nology of pro'duction means you need 'very 'little 'labour 'input. I'm 'holding in my hand a 'simple pen that 'British 'Airways gives a'way to its 'passengers. It is made in 'Switzerland, a pen, a 'low-tech 'product, made in 'Switzerland, with the 'highest 'labour costs in the en'tire world, and 'British 'Airways, a 'British 'company, 'having to pay in low 'value pounds, is 'buying from 'Switzerland a manu'factured 'product. Now what's 'going on here? It seems to me that the Swiss – and they 'also 'manage to do it with their 'watches, the 'famous Swatch – have 'stumbled on a new 'secret, which is how to make 'low-tech 'products, sell them 'profitably, but 'actually make them in a 'country where in 'theory there should be no more manu'facturing, and if you look at 'any of the suc'cessful e'conomies of the 'nineteen-'nineties they all have a strong manu'facturing com'ponent.

Exercise 6

administer	**administration**	administrative	
	administrator		
classify	classification	classified	unclassified
		classifiable	**unclassifiable**
develop	**development**	developed	**underdeveloped**
	developer	developing	
		developmental	
innovate	**innovation**	**innovative**	
	innovator		
plan	**plan**	planned	unplanned
	planner		

Exercise 7

Possible sentences include:

There was an abrupt deflation in 1930 and 1931, when prices fell by about 8%.

Inflation rose sharply in 1933.

The price index rose dramatically in 1941.

The big surge in inflation in the mid-1940s was followed by an equally sharp decrease.

There was another big peak in inflation in the second half of the 1940s.

Inflation stabilized at about 1% during the early 1960s.

There were substantial rises in inflation after both the oil shocks in the 1970s.

Inflation tumbled in the early 1980s, from 13% to 1%.

Vocabulary note In French, the adjective *dramatique* is only used for negative things (such as a dramatic decrease in profits). In English, *dramatic* and *dramatically* are neutral, and can be used to describe both positive and negative events.

Exercise 8

Bangladeshi	Belgian	Ethiopian	Irish	Korean
Lebanese	Moroccan	Norwegian	Peruvian	Turkish

Exercise 9

Afghan	Czech	Greek	Filipino
Dutch	Swiss	Thai	Welsh

Note In some cases in Exercises 10–12, other tense or aspect forms (future or past or perfect) would also be possible.

Exercise 10

1 Three of the bank's employees were accused yesterday of buying shares while in possession of inside information.

2 The treasurer admitted to losing / that he had lost $10,000 of the company's money in a Las Vegas casino.

3 The consultants advised the company to restructure its middle management.

4 The management agreed to show the documents to the trade union representatives.

5 Buying just one ordinary share will allow you / its holder to vote at the Annual General Meeting.

6 The production manager apologized for arriving late for the meeting.

7   I have arranged to come back at short notice if any problems arise during my holiday.
8   Because of the cash flow crisis, the company attempted to borrow a further $100,000.
9   The company's staff were asked to avoid speaking to journalists.
10 We are not aware of losing any customers because of these delays.
11 The company believes in distributing profits among both staff and shareholders.
12 Quality problems were blamed for the company losing 20% of its market share.
13 The new factory must be capable of producing a range of different products.
14 I hate fog. I can't stand waiting for hours at airports.
15 Despite the mixed market research reports, we are going to carry on developing this product.
16 The R&D department complained about losing 10% of its budget.
17 Rather than diversifying, we are going to concentrate on making our traditional products.
18 I would like to thank all of you for contributing to increasing our sales this past year.
19 OK, you have convinced me to stay with the company.
20 We cannot count on remaining market leader for ever.

Exercise 11

1   We have delayed introducing the product until the New Year.
2   The advertising department denied misleading the public about the product.
3   Because of our huge advertising budget, competitors are deterred from entering the market.
4   This joint venture will enable us to enter the Chinese market.
5   Do you really enjoy working 50 hours a week?
6   The company failed to increase its sales in the first quarter of the year.
7   The government wants to forbid companies [from] advertising alcoholic products on television.
8   I forgot to arrange the meeting with the suppliers.
9   Many middle managers say they are frightened of losing their jobs.
10 We'll probably give up sending publicity material to schools and universities.
11 We guarantee to provide free after-sales service for two years.
12 You had better check those figures before the meeting on Monday.
13 The new law should help investors [to] understand a company's financial situation more easily.
14 You really ought to enquire about joining the employers' association.
15 The union representative insisted on speaking to the managing director.
16 The company is interested in expanding into Latin American markets.
17 The marketing department is keen on increasing the proportion of sales on credit.
18 We intend to let each subsidiary decide for itself.
19 In the hope that my proposition will interest you, I look forward to / am looking forward to hearing from you.
20 The law on partnerships is designed to make professional people act responsibly.

Exercise 12

1   Would you mind sharing an office with Mr Vile?
2   We all have to participate in improving the quality of our customer service.
3   We are not permitted to use comparative advertising.
4   If you persist in arriving at work at 10 o'clock, your contract will be terminated.
5   Your job is to persuade politicians to accept our industry's proposals.

6 We promise to refund dissatisfied customers within 30 days.

7 The company was punished for breaking health and safety regulations.

8 Two years on, we regret abandoning the North African market.

9 Because of the recession at home, we now rely on making profits abroad.

10 I remember starting work there at the age of 16.

11 Did you remember to post the invitations to the Christmas party?

12 We will probably start producing / to produce the new model within 18 months.

13 We are still struggling to restore sales to their 1999 level.

14 You will never succeed in getting a job with a CV that looks as bad as that.

15 He was suspected of selling information to a rival company.

16 She is used to working late in the evenings, if necessary.

17 I was never trained to operate this machinery.

18 The bank undertakes to buy any bonds for which they cannot find purchasers.

19 She used to work late in the evenings when she ran the development project.

20 I would rather earn less money and have a shorter working week.